# DATA SCIENCE FROM SCRATCH:

THE FIRST BOOK FOR BEGINNERS WITH
TECHNIQUES FOR A SMARTER FASTER WAY
TO LEARN DATA ANALYSIS, DATA MINING, BIG
DATA FOR BUSINESS, ANALYTICS PRINCIPLES
AND MACHINE LEARNING.

# Table of Contents

# Description

As big data and computer science converged both in the development of new and more powerful hardware and storage systems and with the improved development of machine learning systems and artificial intelligence, a new field that is having a large impact on business intelligence was developed. This field is commonly known as data science. Data science is an interdisciplinary subject that brings together three different fields of study. These include computer science, statistics and probability, and business acumen. All three fields lie at the intersection of business intelligence and big data. In this chapter, we are going to get a handle on the field of data science and how it's going to be used with business intelligence in the future.

It might look obvious in hindsight, but when the Internet was invented, it increased the capability of companies to track people. No one could have predicted the way that this would merged with artificial intelligence and statistics in order to drive a new direction in technology. What the emergence of big data did was to bring together many different fields of study and their application in the real world in a new and different way.

In some ways – and for a while - machine learning was a solution looking for a problem. Big data has provided the exact type of problem that machine learning needs in order to work its magic. This marriage is part of what helps create the new field of data science. This is because a large part of the big data that has been generated is contained within the business environment. Therefore, a new need emerged for people with skill sets that would contain knowledge and abilities across multiple fields. In other words, traditionally computer scientists are not people who have business knowledge. In the old world, computer scientists would have been people whose skillset was focused on machine learning and artificial intelligence along with computer programming.

Then on the other side, you would have experts in the business. Businesspeople, including those trained formally in business school, were not the type of people that would have expertise in fields like machine learning. Therefore, they would not be able to even conceive of applying artificial intelligence to solving business problems, including incorporating it within the business intelligence structure.

In addition to all of this, there is a third subset of experts. That is the people from the mathematics realm who are experts in statistics and probability. These people are certainly able to apply their skillsets to a wide variety of problems. But, traditionally speaking, they have not been involved in the study and application of artificially intelligent computer systems.

This guide will focus on the following:

- Tools and Analysis
- Data Mining
- Types, Quality and Data Preprocessing
- Things you must know for machine learning
- Information Mining, Not Just a Method But a Technique
- Environment Setup
- Reinforcement Machine Learning
- Predictive Analytics
- Data Science in Weather Patterns... AND MORE!!!

# Introduction

The advent of big data has changed all this. The first problem began when businesses were collecting myriads of data, but they had no way to do anything with it. It soon became clear that the use of machine learning was the key to solving the big data problem. After the turn of the 21st-century, machine learning began to grow in importance in the use of dealing with big data in the context of business.

This created a new set of needs. Companies that were using big data began to develop a need for expertise across fields, people who could work with machine learning and artificial intelligence applications. These specialists were not needed to make them work, but to understand how to apply them within the business. These people would also need a thorough knowledge of statistics and probability in order to work with the systems, train the systems, and understand the results that they were producing. In order to do that, the expert would have to have B/business knowledge in addition to their other skillsets.

As these things converged, the field of data science was born, and it quickly became official.

## Comparing and Contrasting Data Science and Business Intelligence

First, let's look at what business intelligence is in relation to data. We must admit to ourselves that there is a's definition of business intelligence that is rooted in the past and that it needs to change as we keep evolving in a new situational environment. The main purpose of business intelligence has been to gather the current state of data that is behind the operation of the business for humans to make data-driven business decisions. Although recent efforts have been upgrading traditional business intelligence systems - such as data dashboards - for the most part, business intelligence is rooted in the static view of the business. In short, business intelligence looks at a frozen passed state of the business in order to move forward with new decision-making. This is a completely understandable situation, given the nature of the tools that have been available to businesses in the past. Large databases, and spreadsheets, and so forth, are - by their very nature - rooted in a static picture that is a snapshot of a past state of the data. Therefore, the process of business intelligence is to interpret the past data that has come into the business, and most of that data (if not all that data) has been in the form of structured data. Traditionally speaking business intelligence has been used to drive reporting or the development of spreadsheets which can present data in charts and so forth, that the business can use to interpret and then make decisions about future actions. This type of data has not been used to make predictive decisions for the most part.

So now let's look at what data science is, and how it operates. What we have done so far is to define the major components of data science that are used as tools. Those are machine learning, or artificial intelligence, business knowledge, and statistics. But these are tools, and they should not be confused with data science itself. Data science, like business intelligence, is a data-driven enterprise. However, data science looks to extract hidden patterns, meanings, and insights, from structured and unstructured data. One of the key differences between data science and business intelligence is that data science seeks to either predict future outcomes or to be able to take advantage of unknown patterns in future data.

The naïve observer would look at this and believe that business intelligence and data science are completely different. They seem to have different goals, and they're applied to different situations. They do have some things in common on the surface. That is, both data science and business intelligence are looking to improve the competitive advantages of the enterprise. This can be done across the entire operational procedures of the business. It can impact the allocation of resources, customer service, expansion into markets, increasing efficiency and avoiding wasteful spending, and other things that impact the general efficiency and success of the business. Thus, everyone will agree that to a certain extent, data science and business intelligence can have the same end goals for the company in mind.

However, one should step back and look at what business intelligence really is. The fact is, business intelligence is going to grow and evolve in this new environment, and it will incorporate data science into the business intelligence model and process and use it to help drive not only increasing efficiency, but also actionable decision-making. It is not necessary for upper-level management and senior executives to have detailed understandings about the workings of data science. It is up to the data science team to extract useful information from their activities that can be used for important decision-making by upper-level executives.

It is also a myth that business intelligence must be constrained to using structured data. Data science represents an opportunity to expand business intelligence into a broader framework that can utilize the huge amounts of unstructured data that companies are collecting both externally and internally. We have already described the ways that unstructured information that a company has access to could be used to improve the efficiency of the company massively.

Think about what some of the end goals are business intelligence when it comes to using the data that it does use in a traditional sense. The problem that most analysts have had when it comes to looking at business intelligence is there to focus on the sources of the data in the way that they are presented and utilized by the business. Instead, you should focus on the end results that you would seek to achieve through the application of business intelligence. When you do this, it is easier to adopt a broader horizon within which you can incorporate the tools and sources of data used in data science.

Let's take a concrete example from UPS. It is well known that UPS utilized Machine learning systems in order to identify patterns exhibited by their drivers during day-to-day operations. From this effort, the company was able to identify changes that could be made to reduce fuel consumption across the company. These changes were then implemented. So, if we ignore the source of the data, we can see that this is the kind of problem that we might address using business intelligence, if only we had the information available. The only difference here is one of technology. That is in a traditional sense; the type of data needed to solve this problem simply was not available using the tools that have been traditionally in existence when it comes to Business intelligence. But you can read any business intelligence book or article and find copious examples of how one of the goals of business intelligence is to improve operations in the business — furthermore, decisions made using business intelligence our data-driven decisions.

So, looking at the UPS example, where is the distinction between what the data is telling you and then making a data-driven decision based on it, or saying it is data science or business intelligence?

The reality here is that we are looking out data science in the wrong way. Instead of seeing data science as a distinct entity, we should instead view data science as an additional tool that can be used as part of the overall process of business intelligence. Too many people who are experts in business intelligence are making these mistakes because they are uneducated or lack proper education when it comes to data science. Quite frankly, the understanding of many business intelligence experts of data science is confined to a top-level understanding of it that they glean from reading articles and publications. In fact, we can go so far as to say that some people in the business intelligence community are threatened by data science.

However, when you step back and look at how data science can be used, it's clear that these fears are completely misplaced. There is absolutely no reason for the business intelligence community to try to keep data science outside of it or to even fear it. Instead, it should be embraced and incorporated into the totality of business intelligence.

You will read articles about business intelligence that claim that it can only understand data that is structured and formatted. That is completely absurd.

It is limited thinking that is only viewing business intelligence than the framework of current technologies. Buy an analogy, let's imagine that it's 1975, and the issue is the introduction of electronic computers together with word processors and spreadsheets. If we were using the logic that some in the business intelligence community are using now, you would have said that spreadsheets could play no role in the accounting department, because accountants are working with pencil and paper ledgers. But what happened as spreadsheets were adopted? The accounting process changed and incorporated spreadsheets within it.

This is what is going to happen when it comes to the relationship between business intelligence and data science. The reason that this is going to happen is that data science and business intelligence have the same goals when it comes to meeting the needs of improving the competitive advantages of the business. Furthermore, both data science and business intelligence seek to promote data-based decision-making.

- Also, you should not get caught up in the situation of focusing on the fact that in many cases, artificial intelligence systems are able to work autonomously. That is another side issue that only serves as a distraction. In both cases, this was done using machine learning and data science. It is clear to this author that looking at the results they could be considered to be something that would fit within the overarching realm of business intelligence if you're willing to expand it and update the notion of what business intelligence is going forward into the future.

## Improved Efficiency Through Automation

Remember the V's that we talked about regarding big data? One of the V's was volume, and another was velocity. These two are going to increase exponentially as the years and decades pass. That means businesses are going to be forced into a situation where they need to rely on data science and data scientists in order to interpret and understand the big data that is playing a role in their business.

The intern is going to be increasingly influenced by artificial intelligence and autonomous computer systems. This is only going to serve to increase the efficiency of business intelligence massively. Many aspects of business intelligence that are traditionally done by humans are going to be increasingly automated and made far more efficient. That is going to magnify the power of business intelligence exponentially. It is going to be an incumbent on business intelligence experts to bring themselves up to speed on data science; they will have to increase their understanding of statistics and machine intelligence.

This requirement is often misunderstood and often framed in terms of an either/or situation. That is, we are returning to the view that business intelligence is somehow threatened by data science. But once again, this is a complete misunderstanding. Rather than looking at data science as being competitive to business intelligence and making excuses about people in business intelligence not understanding or being able to understand the workings of data science, we need to be realistic about this.

Does someone in business intelligence understand all the computer code that is behind a database, or the internal workings of spreadsheet programs like Microsoft Excel?

Of course not. What they do understand is the high-level aspects of these tools. So, when it comes to incorporating data science into business intelligence, a high-level understanding of the tools is what is necessary. In this way, data science is going to enhance the ability of those in business intelligence to make it effective and actionable decisions for the business. Once again, we have already seen how this works in practice. Data science is helping companies improve their efficiency, break into new markets, allocate resources effectively, massively expand, and improve their marketing, advertising, customer service, and much more. Let's look at some potential applications a big data and data science that can have exciting uses within the context of better business intelligence.

Until recently, and even in the present for most companies, huge amounts of useful data that can improve internal operations are simply sitting collecting dust on hard drives. Companies need to analyze ways that employees are communicating with each other and using their time in order to improve efficiency.

- We are starting to see this with monitoring systems based on artificial intelligence. Companies are so much as snooping, because you are working on company time, and the organization has every right to see how their employees are using their time and resources. For those companies that have started using these tools, increasing the level of productivity and efficiency among employees has been one of the many benefits to come out of this. It makes it easier to weed out bad employees and makes it possible to bring problems to the attention of good employees, allowing those employees to rectify the situation. By studying the movements of employees, it's also possible to reallocate the positioning of employees in the company to increase the efficiency of collaboration between different groups and employees. This is analogous to views of artificial intelligence in hospital environments wherein nursing staff has been completely redesigned to consider the needs of patients throughout the facilities. So, in the same way, a company that really doesn't understand why it distributes employees among offices the way it does can instead put employees in locations where they are going to be needed most of the time. Until now, the tenancy has been to distribute employees in the building based on the group or department they belong in, considering where any free office space exists. What if instead, you actually studied the data derived from tracking employee movements where they were spending most of their time that was devoted to productive activity and then you brought employees closer together that actually needed to be close together in order to get work done?

# Tools and Analysis

Numerous enterprise Big Data technologies have been created by startups that have discovered some ways to manage massive volumes of data. They have created breakthrough technologies; which organizations can use to gain valuable data and convert into information and then into business wisdom.

Big players in the IT world have also built significant Big Data solutions in recent years, specifically, large companies that like all-inclusive Big Data solution. Moreover, many different forms of analysis could be performed employing these technologies, and every type can provide different results.

As there are Big Data solutions for almost each need and any use in any type of business, we cannot cover them all in this book. Hence, our focus will be on some the most significant areas.

Remember, one flaw of Hadoop is that it only works in groups and so it cannot easily manage massive amounts of data in real-time. But real-time streaming and data processing provides numerous advantages for business organizations.

Some technology vendors in Big Data have developed a layer on top of Hadoop or have completely developed totally fresh tools, which could cope with real-time data storage, processing, analyzing, and visualizing. These tools can now analyze structured and unstructured data in real-time, considerably enhancing the function of MapReduce and Hadoop.

Some of these technologies can combine data from various sources directly in a platform. Hence, they prevent the need for more data warehousing, but can still deliver real-time interactive charts, which are easy to control and make sense of.

Some vendors are now concentrating on delivering the final visual representation of Big Data. Visualizing structured and unstructured data is needed to convert data into information, which can be challenging. However, new Big Data companies seem to understand the importance of data visualization and have created different solutions suited for organizations.

Most visualizations are designed to appeal to the human eyes that improve the capacity of our brain to detect patterns. This strategy makes the data easy to read and understand. Using different colors and graphics will allow the audience to easily detect patterns and recognize anomalies.

Another form of data visualization is a strategy known as topological analysis that concentrates on the shape of data and could recognize clusters and statistical significance. Data professionals usually use this to discover natural patterns in clusters. This form of analysis is best visualized with three-dimensional clusters, which show the topological spaces and could be interactively explored.

It is certainly not always important to have innovative, complex, and interactive visual representations. Infographics are visual representations of data, information, or knowledge, which could help complex and difficult material easier to digest. Dashboards integrating various data streams showing conventional graphs (bar, pie, line, or column) could also offer valuable insights.

There are instances that real-time updated basic graphs showing the status of processes could actually offer more valuable insights to aid in decision making than more innovative and complex visualizations. On handheld devices, visualizations could be interpreted in a new context when a user can play interactively with the data while pinching, zooming, swiping, or rotating.

Even though the ability to visually represent real-time analytics in an attractive manner can be helpful, it is even more important for business organizations to be able to project future results.

This is largely different from current business intelligence that normally looks at what has already occurred using analytical tools that may not help you predict the future. Predictive analytics can help organizations to consider actionable intelligence according to the same data.

Hence, numerous Big Data startups are focusing on predictive modeling abilities, which will enable companies to be ready on what may come. Gathering as much data as possible while a potential customer is visiting an online store can provide valuable information.

Insights such as pages browse, and products viewed, transactional information or session insights could be integrated with historical and comprehensive customer information about past purchases and loyalty program files.

This offers a whole picture about the visitor and could help in projecting the probability of the visitor to become a paying customer. With these insights, businesses can take necessary actions.

Predictive analysis is often used in e-commerce to aid customers purchase electronics, buy airline tickets, or reserve hotel rooms.

These services could aid customers buy products at the right price and at the right moment by notifying customers when prices are about to drop or what the best day of the week to shop.

In any industry, predictive analysis can be of great use, but it can be a keystone online strategy for insurance companies. This type of analytics can be used to identify which policy-holders are more likely to file claims and to estimate the risk the organization is facing. Predictive analysis works better with more data collection, because the algorithm may consider more variables for its projections.

Targeting potential customers is easier through profiling. The ultimate objective is to build a complete view of every customer so that a specific segment of once could be developed. Behavioral analysis could be used to determine patterns in structured and unstructured data across customer journeys. This will provide the organizations the ability to better understand their customers.

Customer patterns sourced from data like geographic, economic, demographic, and psychographic, can help companies to better understand their target market. Marketing and sales data like operations insights, campaign data, and conversion information, will also provide companies with precise information about their customers, which could be used to increase customer acquisitions and retention, increase cross-selling and upselling, and improve online conversion.

Customer profiles could also be employed in networks that make recommendations, which are quite common in Big Data. The most popular application for recommendation is the engine used by Amazon that allows users to receive personalized homepage when they are visiting the online store.

But retail is not the only industry that can use recommendation network to encourage customers to purchase more products. Recommendation networks are also applicable in other industries and they have different applications.

Recommendation networks are often based on two various types of algorithms, which are usually integrated. The first analyzes massive amounts of data about past purchases or choices of customers and utilizes this data for product suggestions. This is known as collaborative filtering, which is a system to recommend other products according to what other users who have the same profile have purchased.

For instance, a customer purchased W, X, Y and Z and another customer purchased V, W, X, Y, and Z. The engine will suggest product V to the first consumer because they have similar purchasing patterns. The second strategy is based on content filtering, wherein the engine utilizes a comprehensive profile of what a user has purchased in the past sessions, searched for, liked, blogged about, tweeted, websites visited, and much more.

Relying on this insight, a profile could be generated and products are suggested that can best fit this profile according to certain product attributes.

Many customers are familiar with recommendation systems from online stores, but they can also be used for B2B businesses, for instance, to suggest possible prospects to sales team. Public data sets like credit bureau profiles could be integrated with an organization's own sales and customer database to look for new relationships that a salesperson might have overlooked.

Hence, recommendation engines are becoming more common in insurance and finance companies, where they are used to recommend, on top of many benefits, sales strategies, or investment opportunities.

As a matter of fact, recommendation networks could be used anywhere consumers are searching for products or services or people. For instance, LinkedIn is now using recommendations to recommend groups, jobs, or people you may want to connect with. This suggestion function combines collaborative and content-based filtering and employs graph-based and algorithmic approach for suggestions.

Developing a digital profile of every group and identifying the most representative features of this group's members builds recommendations. LinkedIn suggests jobs by integrating various profile features like location, behavior, and attributes of connections that are similar to yours.

If you have already noticed, recommendations have now become a regular feature for many large websites, from e-commerce stores to travel pages. For any business working with suggestions, the technique is to provide relevant suggestions. This can enhance the customer experience and improve the conversion rate.

With the growing volume of data, recommendation networks will only be developed in the future. For businesses, this could mean improved targeting of products to the right individual and so, possibly an increase in the conversion rate. For customers, this will help them to easily find products that they are searching for. But this can also have a disadvantage.

If the recommendation network becomes so good and suggests services or products before consumers are even aware of them, how will this affect the possibility of a user discovering products that they are not really interested? Businesses must be aware of this, as there is a possibility that this could backfire.

The recommendations will improve if websites start using machine-learning engines for real-time suggestions because the engine will learn from recommendations that are not successful. The numerous social networks today can also create a vast amount of data about customers. Likes, Tweets, check-ins, blog posts, and comments can provide organizations answers to crucial questions like:

- What is the sentiment of my customers about my brand?

- What is the perception of my customers to my new product line?

- How can products or services be further improved for customer satisfaction?

Businesses that are using natural language processing and deep machine engines can easily interpret the meaning of comments on social media networks and add generic statements into the right mix. Social media analytics could help businesses to better understand their customers.

Once combined with other tools like usage logs, support tickets, surveys, sales data, and other sources of customer intelligence, social media analytics could convert customer retention into a data-oriented process, which will improve conversion and reduce attrition.

Segmentation and clustering analysis is a data-focused strategy to search for patterns within vast volumes of data and to cluster data sets that are alike. This goes much beyond the human-generated segments that are usually based on traits that are easy to identify like gender, age, and location.

Big Data segmentation and clustering performed by algorithms could look for patterns and segments that will otherwise stay concealed. In using self-learning engines, the segmentation will be enhanced. On the other hand, segmentation will allow the engine to learn more about the segmentation it generates.

For example, it could generate with clusters of customers who are about to become parents in a certain location in a specific type of job, and in a specific age group. The result could be used to push targeted and personalized marketing campaigns.

Whatever could be discovered in the Big Data could be converted into a segment, and this could help businesses to better improve their products or services.

Outliers could be shown where clusters could be discovered. By looking for the outlier within Big Data and determining the special exception, a business could discover unexpected insights. Even though looking for an outlier can be extremely challenging, it can be easier with the use of algorithms. These abnormalities could have excellent value if they are discovered.

One example is detecting fraud or determining criminal activities in electronic banking. With self-learning algorithms and machine learning, detecting an outlier could search for correlations that are not easy to understand for humans because of the vast volumes of data needed for identifying the pattern.

In similarity search, an algorithm will try to look for an object, which is most similar to the object of interest. A good example of this is the application Shazam that can look for a song in a database containing around 12 million songs after only listening for several seconds.

Just a few years ago, SQL queries are done to search for the components that are matching specific conditions like "search all Toyota cars for sale in Kansas City". Because these algorithms are using Big Data to look for similarities, there is a high probability to succeed in finding what you are specifically looking for.

More often than not, algorithms could also run thousands of searches simultaneously in a few seconds, thereby getting results immediately.

There are now Big Data companies that are concentrating on the aspect of human capital. Based on a report from McKinsey, about 190,000 data scientists will be needed in the United States by year 2018. If Big Data can be made easier to control and organize, this concern could be addressed by eliminating the need for expensive hires.

Exploring and accessing heterogeneous data could be made so basic that users can be able to integrate Big Data sources that are stored, for instance, on Hadoop on conventional sources and do analyses on them without the need to be a specialist in data science.

There are tools that are already available in the market designed for small and medium enterprises who are interested to try Big Data strategy without spending too much, especially on hiring specialists and buying IT equipment.

The tools provide these organizations with one platform, which incorporate data from any source in any setting and allows them to perform analyses or build integrated data views. But the problem is that it can be a challenge to adapt the solution to personal needs. For comprehensive Big Data solutions, engineers and scientists will always be indispensable.

# Data Mining

When confronted with large data sets, it is important to get relevant information from the data. This process goes by the name data mining in some contexts. Data mining is the process of examining big data to find the patterns it contains. There are many aspects involved in data mining, including regression analysis, detecting anomalies in the data, using machine learning, and clustering. We will examine these factors in this chapter and explore the concept of data mining.

Data mining can be applied to almost any industry. Some industries where it has already been used extensively include banking and finance, personally tailored marketing, detection of spam email, and fraud detection in general.

Raw data is often highly disorganized. To utilize it, an organization must have staff on hand that can access the data, do some preliminary analysis, and organize it in useful and productive ways. There are several weak points in the process of data mining, but they are easy to manage effectively with a little planning. Although artificial intelligence and machine learning, along with raw computational power in general, will play a large role in data mining, the human element remains a crucial part of the process.

## Data Mining: What Is It?

Data mining is just another way to describe the process of finding hidden patterns that exist in large data sets. Multiple methods can be utilized to discover these patterns. These include using the methods of statistics and tools like regression to help researchers build a relationship between input and output data. Machine learning often plays a central role in the process of data mining because machine learning is often far more effective than human analysis regarding extracting hidden patterns within data sets.

Several core elements must be in place to use data mining. The first of these is either an effective method of data collection or the ability to obtain data from third-party sources. Second, you must have warehousing in place, which essentially involves the ability to store all this data. Cloud computing has made this capacity accessible even to small businesses. Next, it is important to have the required computer processing power. These form the core components that can then be used in conjunction with machine learning algorithms to produce models for predicting future outcomes.

The main point regarding data mining is that it grew out of efforts to find patterns in data without using any hypothesis of what those patterns might be beforehand.

The purpose of data mining is the same purpose that lies behind many, if not most, uses of big data. That is, you want to use data mining to make future predictions. For businesses, this can help them retain customers, improve service, cut operational costs, increase product reliability and safety, and more.

Data mining was originally used with databases, so is most closely associated with structured data. It was one of the first efforts that grew out of modern computer technology calling upon interdisciplinary skills. These include computer science, using artificial intelligence and machine learning, along with statistics and probability. As computing power has increased over the years and costs have declined, the ability to use data mining has increased and expanded.

In the past, researchers had to do much manual work, developing models that would essentially be educated guesses, and then writing software to go through the data and do the work. However, machine learning has changed this process. Now manual work has been minimized, restricted to choosing the type of model to use and selecting data sets that can be incorporated in training the artificially intelligent system. Then the computer can do all the work, learning from the data and rapidly finding hidden connections and patterns that were previously unknown to the business or organization.

While early data mining efforts were focused on structured data, things have changed a lot in the past twenty-five years. Unstructured data now makes up an estimated 90 percent of all data collected. With unstructured data, there is more potential for discovering hidden information, so this data can be extremely useful.

However, unstructured data also presents many important problems. From the point of view of a human observer, this data is noisy. This is why machine learning can play a large role in modern data mining efforts. Machine learning makes it possible to sift through the apparent noise and chaos and do it in a relatively fast period. This allows organizations of various types to gather important information from their data, including previously hidden correlations and trends. Data mining is used in conjunction with predictive analytics to develop effective predictive models that can be enforced to future data to predict possible outcomes.

## Data Mining Software

Many software tools are specifically designed for data mining purposes. The software can be used to classify data and group it into useful clusters for future analysis. This will be used in conjunction with data warehousing, which is the process of storing and analyzing the data. Usually, the data is collected from multiple sources. Data warehouses can run queries on the data as well as do analysis, but one of the main functions of data warehousing is to store the data electronically so they can be accessed. This process can involve consolidating data from different sources and using analysis to extract relevant data that can be used for predictive analytics and other purposes. Data mining is the process of looking for patterns in the data.

## Descriptive Modeling

Several techniques used in data mining fall under the umbrella of descriptive modeling. The goal of descriptive modeling is to use past data that has been collected to uncover factors that played a role in the failure or success of products, services, and activities. Several techniques are utilized in descriptive modeling to improve future outcomes by producing more products that are reliable and help to improve the match of company services to customer desires.

Clustering

The first technique we will examine in this process is called clustering, which forms "clusters" of objects or data points that share certain characteristics. For example, in a customer database, you might develop clusters of customers by gender and age. One cluster might be females aged thirty-five to forty. Clusters are used with data mining to develop an exploratory process that might find important correlations in the data. Statistics play an important role in developing

42

the appropriate clusters. The idea is to get a group of data that has more similarities than differences as compared to other clusters.

The type of data does not have to be structured or related to people, so the example above is just one such example. Clustering could be used in image analysis or other applications where the data is unstructured and impersonal. When building clusters, scientists use a distance function defined for the specific problem at hand. The concept will be an abstract one for most applications, but it is mathematically similar to the standard distance functions used in algebra and basic physics. It turns out that "distance" is a general concept, and if you have the right data points to examine, you can determine an abstract distance not based on physical location but based on characteristics and properties that can help you find similar or different data points. To use it properly, a distance threshold would have to be defined to determine the membership in one cluster or another for a specific data point.

One way this could be used is in grouping pixels together to form an image. Rather than grouping them by their location in the image, you might group them by color instead. For example, you can set a threshold to determine whether a pixel qualifies as "red," "green," "blue" etc., and then in your data analysis, you would group them in this fashion, again ignoring other properties like image location. An alternative examination could develop different clusters of the data. You could look at the brightness of each cluster instead, and group pixels according to different levels of brightness.

## Anomaly Detection

Anomaly detection looks for data points that are outliers. The definition of an outlier must be precisely defined, but anomaly detection is a very important tool used in data mining because outliers often represent important problems. There is always noise in the data, so errors must be quantified. One obvious application of anomaly detection is using medical scans such as a CT scan or MRI, that might discover differences in tissue density and so forth that could be caused by the presence of a tumor or foreign object.

Anomaly detection is also important for detecting fraud. When there are data points that are outliers, this is often a strong indication that something is awry.

Anomalies can take many forms. It might take the form of data far outside the norm. However, it could also take the form of an unusual frequency of data. Often, when people are trying to break into computer networks, this could result in a spike in access attempts.

Anomaly detection can be used to detect spam emails. This can be based on the method of contact or the content of the message. For example, emails that demand payment or that ask the user to reveal certain important personal information can be flagged as anomalies.

Machine learning can play a central role in anomaly detection. One-way machine learning can be trained is to provide the system with input and output data from past experiences that are thoroughly known. For example, the computer system can be fed information related to bank fraud, which could include inputs of various types together with outputs that indicate either normal transactions or fraudulent transactions. By studying the inputs and outputs, the machine can learn how to appropriately tune various parameters to accurately predict the outcomes of future events.

Sometimes that type of data is not known, or we want the computer to find hidden anomalies. Large data sets can be passed into the system. Presumably, most data collected is "normal." Most banking data, for example, will involve perfectly normal and legal transactions that do not involve any kind of fraud. Maybe one case out of a thousand is fraudulent. You let the system work on large data sets to learn what is normal and what is not.

Typical applications of anomaly detection include network intrusion or hacking attempts, spam email, insurance fraud, loan application and bank fraud, tax fraud, and unusual activity detected with sensor networks. Anomaly detection is also used for data security, with mixed results so far.

Many techniques are used in fraud detection. First off, remember that this kind of work will be probability-based. Therefore, the techniques of statistics are often brought to the problem. In some cases, fraud will be missed, and in others, there will be false positives. Bayesian networks can help maximize the probability of success. Clustering can also be used since grouping data points will reveal outliers that are classified according to a certain distance level. Nearest neighbor techniques are also useful in detecting outlying data points.

## Association Rules

Another task performed during data mining is to look for hidden relationships between the data. There are many applications of this. For example, you might analyze data of women aged thirty-five to forty to see what drinks they order with what types of food in restaurants. Or you might determine what shoes they purchase on Amazon while purchasing clothing items. All kinds of associations may exist in data.

Classification

The classification problem generally involves sorting data into bins. The simplest classification problem will be one that is binary in nature. You could analyze customers of your cell phone network and classify whether they are Android or iOS users. One of the most famous classification problems is that of detecting spam email. By searching for characteristics and text snippets that are commonly used in spam email, the system can use an either-or method to classify an email as spam or not. In the real world, this must be done on a threshold basis. An email might show 45 percent of the known characteristics of a spam message. In that case, it would be classified as not spam if the threshold were set to 50 percent. A message with 55 percent would definitely be classified as spam. However, these types of detection methods are obviously not perfect, which is why even though it has gotten better over the years, email systems still commit frequent errors with this task.

Regression

Regression is a technique that attempts to get data into an input-output relationship of the form

$$y = f(x)$$

Given inputs x, which could be a vector, you get outputs y. By examining large amounts of data, a computer system can fit the data to an equation or sets of equations to make predictions when presented with future input data. If the data set is suitable for this type of analysis, the training will probably involve what is called labeled data. The labeling is that the data is labeled as input or output, and the computer is exposed to known answers so it can start learning the parameters involved in the relationship. These are tuned and then if the data set is large enough, they are likely to be highly accurate.

In the past, people had to make educated guesses with parameters in the equations, and repeatedly test and adjust until they arrived at the right answer through manual work. Now, this can be done with real-time adjustments made by the computer system itself with the machine learning process.

## Knowledge Discovery in Databases (KDD)

This is a staged way to go about finding patterns in data. Data mining is part of this process, but it is not the only aspect of KDD. The process begins with selecting the appropriate data. Humans working on the problem usually do this. It is a very important step; if the wrong data is selected, then you are getting off on the wrong foot.

The data must then go through a stage of pre-processing. This necessary step must be performed for data mining algorithms to work correctly and will involve some judgment. Researchers may have access to very large data sets, or, in some cases, they may not have large amounts of data. Either way, this would be problematic. Although, strictly speaking, more data

# Types, Quality and Data Preprocessing

Through this chapter the user understands that data, types and their quality are an integral part of the data mining process. It becomes clear that data quality determines to a great extent the quality of the data mining results. The data parameters which affect their quality should be clear in order to be able to be evaluated and optimized by a user. Data preprocessing is the hardest and most time-consuming part of the Knowledge Discovery in Databases process.

The goal of this chapter is to familiarize the user with all different forms of data preprocessing and make him able to apply them. Also make the user able to apply these techniques through a tool, like the R programming language.

## Types, Quality and Data Preprocessing

Data preprocessing is one of the most important steps of Knowledge Discovery in Databases, which might need up to the 60% of the total effort. This happens because if data are not clean and in the right form, then there is no point in discussing about results quality. Later on, we will discuss the basic categories and types of variables which a dataset can have. Additionally, we will discuss from which processes preprocessing consists of and when to use each one and we will also view some examples. Last, we will present the *dplyr* and *tidyr* packages of R which are used to manage and clean data respectively.

## Categories and Types of Variables

The two basic variable categories are the qualitative and the quantitative.

Qualitative variables refer to variables, like gender, level of education, location etc. They are divided in nominal and ordinal (or tactical). Nominal variables represent categories, of which the order does not matter like e.g. color. Conversely, ordinal or tactical variables represent categories, of which the order does matters, e.g. disease severity.

Quantitative variables are numerical values, expressed in a unit of measure e.g. age. They are divided in discrete and continuous variables. Depending on the unit of measure, data can be characterized as categorical. On the image below, we can view briefly all categories and variable types.

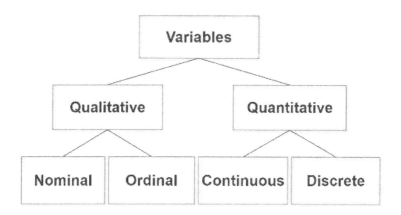

## Preprocessing processes

That's why data should be preprocesses in order to ensure their quality. Below we will view the most basic processes used during data preprocessing.

### Data cleansing

The most important actions of data cleaning are:

- filling out missing values
- finding outliers and smoothing, as long as they contain noise
- fixing any data inconsistencies

## Missing Values

Data are not always available. More specifically, in many rows of the dataset, values may not be available. This is what we call missing values. It can be caused by many different things like equipment malfunction, inconsistencies with other recorded data which led to their deletion or simply data which were never stored. In any case, we might need to assume missing data and fill them out.

The first step in handling missing data is to identify the rows with missing values. Then we should fill them out. Obviously, if the dataset is huge, this process cannot be done manually. The easiest solution is to ignore this particular row. Though If we have a huge number of missing values, this is not a very effective solution.

Some of the most effective, automated solutions for filling out missing values are the following:

- use of global constant for filling out missing values e.g. -1, "unknown", new class
- use of the average of the feature for filling out missing values

- use of the average of samples of the same class for filling out missing values
- use of the most probable value for filling out missing values, produced by some method like decision trees, regression etc.

## Data with Noise

Although data could be available, they might have noise or outliers in them.

There are many ways to handle data with noise. We will focus on the methods of binning and clustering. Data classification is the first step of every binning method, so that later on they can be split into bins. Based on how they are split into bins, they are distinguished in equal width partitioning (distance) methods and equal depth partitioning (frequency) methods.

During equal width partitioning, the range is divided in N intervals of equal size. This partitioning though is prone to outliers since non-symmetrical data are not handled properly. During equal depth partitioning, the range is divided in N intervals which contain the same number of samples. In this case we have better data scaling. Binning methods are used for discretization as well. The most known are:

- Regularization based on the average value of each bin: values are replaced with the average of each bin
- Regularization based on the median of each bin: values are replaced with the median of each bin
- Regularization by using the limits of each bin: values are replaced with the value of the limits, depending on which limit is closer

*Example – Data smoothing using binning methods*

Let's assume we are given some temperatures ($C_o$) in ascending order: 4, 9, 11, 16, 21, 23, 24, 24, 27, 30, 32, 35. By using equal depth partitioning we have the following bins:

Bin 1: 4, 9, 11, 16
Bin 2: 21, 23, 24, 24
Bin 3: 27, 30, 32, 35

Using regularization based on the average of each bin:

Bin 1: 10, 10, 10, 10

Bin 2: 23, 23, 23, 23

Bin 3: 31, 31, 31, 31

Using regularization based on the limits of each bin:

Bin 1: 4, 4, 16, 16

Bin 2: 21, 24, 24, 24

Bin 3: 27, 27, 35, 35

The use of clustering has the goal of grouping data in clusters, so that data with noise can be separated from clean data. In the image below, we can see that three clusters are created and the outliers don't belong to any cluster.

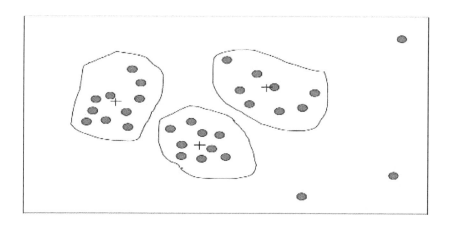

## Inconsistent data

We get inconsistent data when one or more different sources of files have different editions of stored data, which should be the same. In other words, when for the same entity, the values of the features from different sources differ, then we can say that an inconsistency occurs. This usually happens when we have lots of data and we need to make a change. Then it is quite possible to edit one or more files but not all of them. Another possible reason is the different way of presenting or using different scales e.g. units of measures, different currency. For solving the inconsistent data problem, we can either make manual edits by using external sources or semiautomatic edits by using commercial data scrubbing tools or data auditing tools.

## Data Unification

The goal of data unification is to combine data from multiple sources in a coherent edition. When data are stored in databases, schema integration should be applied by using metadata contained from various sources. During the unification process all possible conflicts or inconsistencies between data values should be tracked and analyzed.

Redundant data appear often when multiple databases are unified.

Possible problems which might appear during the unification process are the use of different names across different databases or when an attribute is created by other attributes in different tables. In order to track redundant data association analysis is used.

Finally, it's worth mentioning that by carefully unifying data we can remove unnecessary information, prevent inconsistencies, improve the data mining process and increase the quality of its results.

**Data Transformation and Discretization**

The basic goal of data transformation is to create comparable data which initially were non-comparable. With data transformation we can achieve other positive results like reducing data size.

Discretization can be considered a special type of data transformation. The basic idea is to transform a continuous range in discrete values. Later on, we will see that discretization is necessary for applying some data mining methods.

*Data Transformation*

Data transformation is mostly used for:

- smoothing data and removing noise
- data aggregation
- normalization, scaling the features of a dataset into a specific range
- creating new features from existing ones

The most frequent implementations of data transformation are normalization and creation of new features from existing ones. Normalization is very useful in categorization problems and also when data has different scales and units of measure. There are many different ways of data normalization. The most important ones are the following:

- min-max normalization: values are normalized so that their range belongs to a new limited range e.g. [-1, 1], [0, 10] etc. The new value is calculated by using the following formula:

$$v_{new} = \frac{v - m}{s}$$

- z-score normalization: values are normalized by using the average value and standard deviation so that data have an average value of 0 and a standard deviation of 1. This type of normalization is accomplished with the following formula:

Where m is the average value of the feature and s is its standard deviation.

- Regularization with decimal scale: values are normalized with order of magnitude of 10. Regularization is accomplished with the formula:

$$v_{new} = \frac{v}{10^j}$$

- where j is the smallest integer so that:

$$\max(v_{new}) < 1$$

## Example – Data Regularization

Assume we are given a dataset with ages and heights of students. We want to normalize both two features on the range [0.1].

```
> # Initial dataset
> mydf
  age height
1  15    172
2  23    185
3  12    130
4  32    178
>
> # Finding each column maximum
> M <- sapply(mydf, max)
> M
  age height
   32    185

>
> # Finding each column minimum
> m <- sapply(mydf, min)
> m
  age height
   12    130
>
> # Regularization in the range [0, 1]
> mydf$age <-( (mydf$age - m[1])/(M[1] - m[1])
+ )* (1 - 0) + 0
> mydf$height <-( (mydf$height - m[2])/(M[2] -
m[2])
+ ) * (1 - 0) + 0
>
> mydf
    age      height
1 0.15  0.7636364
2 0.55  1.0000000
3 0.00  0.0000000
4 1.00  0.8727273
>
```

*Data Discretization*

Discretization is associated with 3 type of features:

- nominal features, where values have no intrinsic order
- ordinal features, where values are in a clear order
- continuous features, where all values are real numbers

A discretization example is the sampling from a range or a continues feature. Discretization's main reason of existence is that some classification algorithms receive only categorical features. It can also contribute in the decrease of the number, therefore the data size. For a given continuous feature we can separate its range in intervals and assign labels in each interval as seen below. For example, a value which belongs in the range {k1, k2) will be replaced by the label d2.

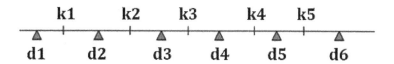

One more discretization technique, is Entropy-based discretization. Assume we have a sample set named S. If S is split into two intervals named S1 and S2, using the threshold T for the values of a feature named A, then the information gain from this split would be:

$$I(S,T) = \frac{|S_1|}{|S|}E(S_1) + \frac{|S_2|}{|S|}E(S_2)$$

Where the entropy function named E for a given set is calculated based on the classification of the sample class in the set. If we have m classes, the entropy for the interval S1 is:

$$E(S_1) = -\sum_{i=1}^{m} p_i \log_2(p_i)$$

Where $p_i$ is the probability of the class i in S1.

The process is applied retrospectively in splits until a termination criterion is met e.g.

$$G(S,T) = E(S) - I(S,T) \leq d$$

Where d is a very small number. In other words, this process is applied retrospectively until we have no more additional gain from further splits. Experiments have shown that discretization can reduce the data size, improving the classification accuracy.

# Example – Entropy-based discretization

On the below table, we see a dataset with the hours studied for an exam and if students managed to pass this exam (Y=Yes, N=No)

| Hours Studied | Success |
|---|---|
| 4 | N |
| 5 | Y |
| 8 | N |
| 12 | Y |
| 15 | Y |

The hours Studied is the continuous variable. We want to discretize our data. We start by calculating the entropy of the whole data. We have three Y (yes) and two N (no). So:

$$E(S) = -\left(\frac{3}{5}\log_2\left(\frac{3}{5}\right) + \frac{2}{5}\log_2\left(\frac{2}{5}\right)\right) = 0.529 + 0.442 = 0.971$$

Next, we need to find which split will give us the maximum gain. In order to find a split, we calculate the average of two neighbor values. For example, from the first two values we get 5+4=9 and T=9/2=4.5. So, the first possible split is at T=4.5. Based on this split we get the following values:

|  | Success | Failure |
|---|---------|---------|
| <=4.5 | 0 | 1 |
| >4.5 | 3 | 1 |

We calculate entropy for each case and the gain of this particular split.

$$E(S_{\leq 4.5}) = -\left(\frac{1}{1}\log_2(1) + 0\log_2(0)\right) = 0 + 0 = 0$$

$$E(S_{>4.5}) = -\left(\frac{3}{4}\log_2\left(\frac{3}{4}\right) + \frac{1}{4}\log_2\left(\frac{1}{4}\right)\right) = 0.311 + 0.5 = 0.811$$

So now we have:

$$I(S,4.5) = \frac{1}{5}(0) + \frac{4}{5}(0.811) = 0.6488$$

and the gain from the split is:

$$G(S,4.5) = E(S) - I(S,4.5) = 0.971 - 0.6488 = 0.322$$

Taking the next two neighbor values we now have 5+8=13 and T=13/2=6.5. So, the second possible split is at T=6.5. Based on this split we get the following values:

|          | Success | Failure |
|----------|---------|---------|
| <=6.5    | 1       | 1       |
| >6.5     | 2       | 1       |

We calculate entropy for each case and the gain of this particular split.

$$E(S_{\leq 6.5}) = -\left(\frac{1}{2}\log_2\left(\frac{1}{2}\right) + \frac{1}{2}\log_2\left(\frac{1}{2}\right)\right) = 0.5 + 0.5 = 1$$

$$E(S_{>6.5}) = -\left(\frac{2}{3}\log_2\left(\frac{2}{3}\right) + \frac{1}{3}\log_2\left(\frac{1}{3}\right)\right) = 0.389 + 0.528 = 0.917$$

So now we have:

$$I(S,6.5) = \frac{2}{5}(1) + \frac{3}{5}(0.917) = 0.95$$

and the gain from the split is:

$$G(S,6.5) = E(S) - I(S,6.5) = 0.971 - 0.95 = 0.021$$

Same, we take the next two neighbor values we now have 8+12=20 and T=20/2=10. So, the second possible split is at T=10. Based on this split we get the following values:

|        | Success | Failure |
|--------|---------|---------|
| <=10   | 1       | 2       |
| >10    | 2       | 0       |

We calculate entropy for each case and the gain of this particular split.

$$E(S_{\leq 10}) = -\left(\frac{1}{3}\log_2\left(\frac{1}{3}\right) + \frac{2}{3}\log_2\left(\frac{2}{3}\right)\right) = 0.528 + 0.389 = 0.917$$

$$E(S_{>10}) = -\left(\frac{1}{1}\log_2(1) + 0\log_2(0)\right) = 0 + 0 = 0$$

So now we have:

$$I(S,10) = \frac{2}{5}(0.) + \frac{3}{5}(0.917) = 0.55$$

and the gain from the split is:

$$G(S,10) = E(S) - I(S,10) = 0.971 - 0.55 = 0.421$$

Last, we take the final two neighbor values we now have 12+15=27 and T=27/2=13.5. So, the second possible split is at T=13.5. Based on this split we get the following values:

|          | Success | Failure |
|----------|---------|---------|
| <=13.5   | 2       | 2       |
| >13.5    | 1       | 0       |

We calculate entropy for each case and the gain of this particular split.

$$E(S_{\leq 13.5}) = -\left(\frac{2}{4}\log_2\left(\frac{2}{4}\right) + \frac{2}{4}\log_2\left(\frac{2}{4}\right)\right) = 0.5 + 0.5 = 1$$

$$E(S_{>13.5}) = -\left(\frac{1}{1}\log_2(1) + 0\log_2(0)\right) = 0 + 0 = 0$$

So now we have:

$$I(S,13.5) = \frac{1}{5}(0) + \frac{4}{5}(1) = 0.8$$

and the gain from the split is:

$$G(S,13.5) = E(S) - I(S,13.5) = 0.971 - 0.8 = 0.2$$

From the above calculations we can understand that the third split at T=10 is the best with the highest gain (0.421). After the split, we can continue examining new splits and, once again, choosing the best one. This process can continue until we have no gain from further splits based on a small value for d.

**Data Reduction**

The problem that data reduction is trying to address is huge amount of data needed to be edited, since complex data analysis might need a lot of time to be executed in a whole dataset.

The data reduction process has a goal of creating a reduced representation of the whole dataset, which is quite smaller in size but can also produce the same, or almost the same results.

*Dimension Reduction*

The more dimensions we have, the hardest it is to manage our data and our data are sparser. This phenomenon is also known as the curse of dimensionality. Data reduction's goal is to better manage, understand and visualize data while at the same time it reduces memory usage and the time needed for the execution of data mining and machine learning algorithms. Two basic approaches for dimension reduction are feature selection and feature projection.

With feature selection we choose the minimum number of features from which it is possible to create equivalent or very similar results with the results we would get if we used all features. Ideally, the number of features chosen is much smaller than the initial number of features.

The most known feature projection for data reduction is the Principal Component Analysis, PCA. The feature transformation creates a new feature set, with less dimensions than the initial one, but without reducing its main dimensions. Often, PCA is used for data visualization as well.

Principal Component Analysis works like this: By having N vectors of k-dimensions it finds m ≤ k orthogonal vectors (two vectors x and y are called orthogonal when their inner product space is equal to 0, that is when $x^T y = 0$) which can be used for representing data in the best possible way. Thus, the initial dataset is reduced, or projected, in a new one, which consists of N data vectors upon m basic components. Each data vector is a linear combination of the m principal components vectors. This technique is mostly used when we have a high number of dimensions.

# Things you must know for machine learning

To be successful with machine learning, you must have the right tools in order to work, just like if you were building a house, you would need to skills and the tools required. The following is a list of the required materials to do machine learning.

## *Data*

To start working with your data, you have to have enough data to break it into two categories; training data and test data.

Training data is the data you use in the beginning when you are building your model. When you are first creating your model, you need to give it some data to learn from. With training data, you will already know the independent variables as well as their respective dependent variables. This means that for every input, you will already know the output of your data. From this data, your model will learn to predict the output on its own. Our training data gives us the parameters we need to make predictions. This is the data that our machine learns from.

Test data is the data that the machine gets once you are satisfied with the model, and you see what it does out in the wild. In this data, we only have the independent variables, but no output. With test data, we can see how well our model does at predicting an outcome with new data.

Your training data should account for most of your data; approximately 70%, while your test data is the remaining 30%. In order to avoid bias, make sure that the data you choose for training data and test data is totally random when you split them up. Don't choose which data to use; let it be random. Don't use the same data for training and testing. Start by giving the training data to the machine and examine the relationships between X and Y, then try to see how well your model did.

The most important question to consider during this process is whether your model will still work when it is presented with new data. You can test this by doing cross-validation. This means you will test your model on data you have not used yet. Keep some data to the side that you didn't use during training to see how accurate your model is at the end.

You can also use K-fold validation to check the accuracy of your model. This method is pretty easy to use and generally unbiased. It's a good technique to use when we don't have a lot of data to work with for testing. For K-fold validation, we will break our data into k folds, usually between 5 and 10. Test each fold and see how they performed across all the folds once you are finished with testing. Usually, the larger your number for k is the less biased your test will be.

So far, we have talked about models interpreting data to find meaning and patterns. But what kind of data are we going to use? Where will we get our data, and what is it going to look like?

Data is the most critical component for machine learning. After all, your model will only learn with data, so it's important that you have data that is relevant and meaningful. It came come in many shapes and sizes, structure differently depending on the kinds of data. The more structured the data is, the easier it is to work with. Some data has very little structure, and this data is harder to interpret. Data for facial recognition can be huge and have very little meaning to the untrained eye.

Structured data is more organized. This is the type of data that you will likely use when you are first starting out. It will help you get your feet wet, and you can start understanding the statistic involved in machine learning. Usually, structure data will come in a familiar form that looks something like this, in rows and columns.

This is called a tabular dataset.

| Market Value | num_bedrooms | num_bathrooms | Sq_ft | pool (Y/N) |
|---|---|---|---|---|
| $207,367 | • 4 | • 3 | • 2635 | • N |
| $148,224 | • 3 | • 2 | • 1800 | • Y |
| $226,897 | • 5 | • 3.5 | • 2844 | • Y |
| $122,265 | • 2 | • 1.5 | • 1644 | • N |
| • | • | • | • | • |

Recall that a feature is some measurable characteristic of a variable. In each column in a tabular dataset, we see a feature. This feature is some measurable dimension or attribute. Here we have used data reflecting the market value of a house as a function of the number of bedrooms, the number of bathrooms, square footage, and whether the house has a pool. Our market value is the Y; this is our dependent variable. Our independent variables, or our Xs, are num_bedrooms, num_bathrooms, st_ft, and pool.

In supervised learning, you will already have the Y in your dataset. In this case, it's the market value of the home. With enough of this data in our model, even if we don't know the market value of a house we should be able to predict it if we have the number of bedrooms, the number of bathrooms, square footage, and whether the house has a pool or not. Data that is organized in this way is relatively easy to work with and have multiple independent variables like this makes this an example of the multivariate regression.

*How much data should you use?*

There is no set rule to how much data you will need for your model, but there are guidelines which you should follow. The most important thing is that when you have several independent variables to analyze, then your model will work the best if your data has as many possible combinations of the independent variables as you can get. If you do this, your model will still work even when it encounters a new combination of features that it hasn't seen before. It will have a pretty good way of predicting, even if the combination is completely new.

A good general rule to follow is that you should have about ten times as many respondents as we do independent variables. In the case of our market value example above, we have num_bedrooms, num_bathrooms, sq_ft, and pool. This is four different independent variables, which means we should have at least forty respondents like the ones listed above to create a reliable model.

Having a lot of variables can help us predict the Y more accurately, but that that be costly and make your data harder to process. You must also consider how you are pooling your data. The market values of houses in Los Angeles will be much different than the market values of houses in Cleveland.

It's also important to keep features as relevant as possible. Having multiple variables will help you make a better prediction, but there are variables that may just create bias in the model.

Refer to Scikit learn to see what they recommend for data sizes for certain types of analysis.

But not all data is useful. We often talk about big data, and it might be easy to assume that the more data we have, the better. But that's not always the case. Some data may not be helpful. Certain variables might get in the way and may make it harder to find the true answer.

Preparing the Data

So now you have your data, but how do you get it to a point where it's readable by your model? Data will rarely suit our modeling needs right out of the gate. For our data to be formatted properly, it usually requires a round of data cleaning first. The process of data cleaning is often referred to as data scrubbing.

We might have data that comes in the form of images or emails. We need to rewrite it so that it has numerical values that will be interpretable by our algorithms. After all, our machine learning models are algorithms or math equations, so the data needs to have numerical values for it to be modeled.

You might also have pieces of data that were recorded incorrectly or in the wrong format. There may be variables that you don't need, and you must get rid of. It can be tedious and time-consuming but it's extremely important to have data that will work and can easily be read by your model. It's the least sexy part of being a data scientist.

This is the part of machine learning where you will probably spend most of your time. As a data scientist, you will probably spend about 20% of your time doing data science and the other 80% of your time making sure your data is clean and ready to be processed by your model. We may be combining multiple types of data, and we need to reformat the recordings so that they fit together. First, in the case of supervised learning, pick the variables that you think are most important for your model. If we choose irrelevant variables or variables that don't matter, we may create a bias and could make our model less effective.

A simple example of cleaning or scrubbing data is recoding a response for gender. On your data, you have a column for male/female. Unfortunately, male and female do not have a numerical value. But you can easily change this by making this a binary variable. Assign female = 1 and male =0. Now you can find a numerical value for the effect that being a female has on the outcome of your model.

We can also combine variables to make it simpler to interpret. Let's say you are creating a regression model that predicts a person's income based on several variables. One of the variables is the education level, which you have recorded in years. So, the possible responses for years of education are 1, 2, 3, 4, 5, 6, 7, 8, 9, 10, 11, 12, 13, 14, 15, 16. This is a lot of discrete categories. You could simplify it by creating groups. For example, you could rewrite variables 1, 2, 3, 4, 5, 6, 7, 8 = primary_ed and rewrite 9, 10, 11, 12 = secondary_ed and rewrite 13, 14, 15, 16 = tertiary education. Instead of having twelve categories, you have three. Respondents either have some primary education, secondary education, or some level of post-secondary or college-level education. This is known as binning data, and it can be a good way to clean up your data if it's used properly.

When you are combining variables to make interpretation simpler, you must consider the tradeoff between having more streamlined data and losing some important information about relationships in the data. Consider that in this example, by combining these variables into three groups instead of sixteen, you may be creating bias in your model.

There a lot of factors that could require you to clean your data. Even a misspelling or an extra space somewhere in your data can have a negative impact on your model.

You might have data that is missing. In order to fix this situation, you can replace the missing values with either the mode of the median of that variable. It's possible to remove data with missing values if there are only a few, but this just means you'll have fewer data to use in your model.

# Information Mining, Not Just a Method But a Technique

Web data mining is isolating likely customers out of colossal data accessible on the Internet by performing different ventures. It could be efficient and organized, or crude, contingent upon the utilization of the data. Web data mining should be possible utilizing a basic database program or putting cash in an expensive program.

Begin gathering fundamental contact data of plausible customers, for example, names, locations, landline, and mobile phone numbers, email locations, and training or occupation whenever required.

Truck and CHAID data mining

While gathering data, you will find that tree-molded structures that speak to choices. These determined choices give rules for the characterization of data collected. Correct choice tree techniques incorporate Classification, and Regression Trees additionally know as CART data mining and Chi-Square Automatic Interaction Detection otherwise called CHAID data mining. Truck and CHAID data mining are choice tree procedures utilized for an order of data gathered. They give a lot of principles that could be connected to unclassified data collected in expectation. Truck portions a dataset creating two-way parts though CHAID sections utilizing chi-square tests creating multiway pieces. The truck requires less data arrangement contrasted with CHAID.

Understanding client's activities

Monitor the client's activities like what does the purchases, when does the are buying, for what reason does he purchase, what is the utilization of his purchasing, and so on. Knowing such straightforward things about your client will assist you with understanding the needs of your client better, and subsequently, the procedure of data mining administrations will be more honest, and quality data would be mined. This will build your relations with your client, which would come at the last outcome in an excellent expert relationship.

## Following demography

Mine the data according to demography, reliant on topography just as financial foundation of the business area. You can utilize government statistics as the wellspring of your data gathering. Remembering it, you can proceed with the comprehension of the network existing and therefore, the data required.

## Utilize your casual discussion in serving your customers better

Utilize minute subtleties of your discussion and comprehension with your clients to serve them. If essential, direct reviews, send an expert blessing or utilize some other item that causes you to see better in satisfying client needs. This will expand the holding among you and your client, and you will most likely serve your client better in giving data mining administrations.

Supplement the gather data in a desktop database. More the data is gathered you will find that you can get ready specific templates in encouraging data. Utilizing a desktop database, it is simpler to make changes later on as and when required.

## Looking after protection

While performing, it is essential to guarantee that you or your colleagues are not disregarding security laws in the social affair or giving the data. When trust is lost, you may likewise free the client, since belief is the base of any relationship, let it be a business connection.

# Data Science: The Famous Buzzword of Tech World

Data science is something that is utilized by pretty much every other industry today. Is the inquiry the reason? The appropriate response is all the client situated item creation. The data made by customers and different substances associated with a business is immense. In any case, at that point to comprehend and scan for significance surmising's from them can be troublesome. This is the place data science helps, utilizing different devices and calculations to investigate it and use it for essential purposes.

The primary target of data science is to make an incentive for the business. Furthermore, esteem for business can be made by measuring the market dangers and opportunities on schedule, knowing requests for new items and administrations, and in particular consumer loyalty and maintenance.

## Utilizations OF DATA SCIENCE

It has an assortment of utilization in various businesses. Businesses enjoyed it are:
• Medicinal industry: utilized for gathering and using different patients' data and convenient dispensing reports.

• Retail and trade: different E-business sites utilize consumer loyalty exercises and furthermore for warehousing and coordination.

• Banking and budgetary foundations: one of the pioneers in utilizing it for distinguishing credit hazards and fakes.

• Stimulation and online networking: they use it for getting client bits of knowledge and substance improvement.
• Transportation industry: to comprehend travel experiences, course arranging, and shipment the executives.

Data science is connected in making streamlined web crawlers, recommendatory frameworks, gaming, mechanical autonomy, voice and picture acknowledgment programming, and so on.

## Procedure OF DATA SCIENCE

Data science is a legitimate well-ordered procedure, which takes both time and persistence. Getting reasonable surmising's from large measures of raw data can be troublesome.

Gathering data: includes gathering data from different sources and putting away them in data structures.

Cleaning data: data, for the most part, have heaps of imperfections and holes, these irregularities are to be evacuated and cleaned.

Investigating data: investigating data incorporates breaking down the data utilizing envisioning instruments and factual models to discover significant examples.

Modeling of data: modeling generally includes making calculations utilizing AI to utilize data as a key and prescient device.

Imparting the outcomes: this is the place one needs to translate the inductions and speak with others, so it tends to be utilized for further business necessary leadership.

The most effective method to BE A DATA SCIENTIST
There are two parts of turning into a data researcher:

• Specialized angle
• Business angle
• In a specialized perspective, one ought to be gifted in:

• Arithmetic
• Measurements
• Programming
• Data mining, cleaning, investigating
• SQL databases, C/C++, Java
• Python, R, SAS
• Calculations and data structure
• Hadoop, Apache Flink, Apache Spark, Hive, and so on.
• Database the board
• AI devices and systems.
• Business abilities one ought to have are:
• Introduction abilities

- Communication abilities
- Systematic basic leadership aptitudes
- Critical thinking aptitudes

To be a fruitful data researcher, alongside specialized and business aptitudes, one ought to have an anomaly to see new issues and pose further inquiries and attempt to illuminate them in a diagnostic manner.

# Multiple Facets of Data Science

## What is Data Science?

The data is surrounding us and is running on a continually expanding way as the world is collaborating increasingly more with the web. The ventures have now understood the immense power behind data and are making sense of how it can change the method for working together as well as how we comprehend and experience things. Data Science alludes to the science of translating the data from a specific arrangement of data. As a rule, Data Scientists gather crude data, process it into datasets, and after that utilization it to build factual models and AI models. To do this, they need the accompanying:

Data accumulation structure, for example, Hadoop, and programming dialects, for example, SAS to compose the spin-offs and questions.

Instruments for data modeling, for example, Python, R, Excel, Minitab, and so forth.
AI calculations, for example, Regression, Clustering, Decision-tree, Support Vector Mechanic, and so forth.

## Segments of a Data Science Project

Considering Concepts: The initial step includes meeting with the partners and posing numerous inquiries to make sense of the issues, available assets, added conditions, spending plan, due dates and so forth.

Data Exploring: Many times, the data can be questionable, deficient, repetitive, wrong, or confused. To manage these circumstances, Data Scientists investigate the data by taking a gander at tests and evaluating approaches to fill the spaces or expel the redundancies. This progression may include systems like Data change, Data Integration, Data purifying, Data lessening, and so forth.

Model Planning: The model can be any model, for example, measurable or AI model. The choice differs, starting with one Data Scientist then onto the next, and furthermore as per the current issue. If it is a relapse model, at that point, one can pick relapse calculations, or if it is tied in with orders, at that point characterization calculations, for example, Decision-tree can deliver the ideal outcome.

Model Building alludes to preparing the model with the

goal that it very well may be sent where it's required. Python packages like Numpy, pandas, for the most part convey this progression, and so forth. This is an iterative advance; for example, a Data Scientist needs to prepare the model multiple times.

Communication: The next advance is conveying the outcomes to fitting partners. It is finished by getting ready simple diagrams and charts demonstrating the disclosure and proposed answers for the issue. Devices like Tableau and Power BI are amazingly valuable for this progression.

Testing and working: If the proposed model is acknowledged, at that point it is driven through some pre-production tests, for example, A/B testing, which is tied in with utilizing, state 80% of the model for preparing and rest for checking the measurements of how well it functions. When the model has breezed through the tests, it is sent in the production environment.

## What Should You Do To Become a Data Scientist?

Data Science is the quickest developing profession of the 21st century. The activity is testing and enables the clients to utilize their innovativeness without limit. Businesses are in extraordinary need of gifted experts to chip away at the data they are producing. What's more, that is the reason this course has been intended to prepare students to lead the world in Data Science. Point by point preparing by rumored faculties, multiple assessments, live projects, online classes, and numerous different offices are accessible to shape students as per the mechanical need.

# Environment Setup

In this chapter you will learn all about setting up the appropriate environment for your machine learning needs. Keep in mind that while all you truly need is Python, working with machine learning algorithms and techniques without any other tool would be extremely difficult. That is why in this chapter you will build your machine learning toolkit which includes Python libraries, modules, packages, scientific distributions, and more.

You will learn how to create an optimal environment with the help of modules such as NumPy, Pandas, Jupyter, and how to use tools such as Scikit-learn and TensorFlow to greatly improve your productivity.

## Python Distributions

Before you jump in head first, you should prepare your work environment in order to have an easier time pre-processing and analyzing your data. Working with algorithms, large datasets, and even just programming can be extremely time consuming without the right tools.

Installing Python and various libraries and modules will certainly give you the flexibility and power you need, however, there's an even more efficient way of getting started. The answer is Python scientific distributions. These distributions are Python installations packaged together with a number of tools that machine learners and data scientists need to work with data sets and specific algorithms.

One of the most popular scientific distributions is Anaconda and we will be discussing it briefly in the next section. However, keep in mind that it is only one of the many distributions which contains the modules and tools needed for machine learning. You can always explore as you study in order to find what suits your needs.

## Anaconda

Anaconda is an open source Python scientific distribution which has risen in popularity due to the many useful packages and libraries it contains, along with the fact that it is a free application that anyone can use. There are close to 200 Python packages that come with Anaconda, including NumPy, Scikit-learn, and Pandas, to name a few of the most valuable ones. Furthermore, Anaconda is also a package management application which makes the import and installation of any package or tool a breeze. You can download, install, or remove anything you need and you can also keep everything up to date with the click of a button. You can even setup a virtual environment if you prefer them over working directly on your system.

Anaconda can be downloaded and installed as the basic version or the premium one. Keep in mind that for most projects you won't need anything more than the free version. It includes everything you need for data pre-processing, exploration, or analysis. In addition, it is available for all computer systems, so you shouldn't encounter any issues when moving a project from one system to another.

In order to install or update anything with Anaconda you need to know a set of commands. It would probably be best for you to check the distribution's online documentation in order to familiarize yourself with all of its features. Now, let's go through some basic commands to get you started. Here's how to install a Python package:

conda install < my_package>

The syntax for removing or deleting a package is the same, just replace "install" with the appropriate keyword. Furthermore, you can install, update, or remove multiple packages at the same time instead of going one by one. Here's how that works:

conda install < my_package1 > < my_package2 > < my_package3 > < my_package233>

As for updating packages, you might want to keep all of the ones you install up to date and that might be a tedious operation if you would have to type the name of every single package you have. Here's how you can update everything at once:

conda update --all

Most package managers included with various scientific distributions work the same. If you don't want to use Anaconda for some reason, you can apply everything you learned in this section to any other application. Even the syntax is usually the same.

## Python Toolkit

No machine learning toolkit is complete without a number of modules and libraries. Python is the chosen language in this field because of how easy it is to extend its functionality and push it to the limit. Preparing your work environment with a number of tools is as important as the machine learning tasks themselves.

In this section we will focus on a number of modules and tools that are specifically used in the machine learning field. Some of them are included inside many scientific distributions, however, you need to be aware of them in order to know what to import. Some of the most important tools include Scikit-learn, Pandas, NumPy, and Tensorflow, among many others. Let's briefly discuss the modules and libraries you'll be using and then explore tools like Tensorflow in more detail:

1. Pandas: This is a library that is designed to be used specifically with Python for the purpose of analysing and manipulating data. What defines it is the fact that it gives you functionality to work with numerical tables, as well as time series.

2. NumPy: This is another library meant to be used with Python because it extends the programming language with the ability to

manipulate large multi-dimensional matrices. Furthermore, it provides you with a number of operations and functions that you can use on those matrices.

3. Scikit-learn: This machine learning library is the core of your toolkit. It includes all the machine learning algorithms you will be working with, such as k-means clustering, support vector machines, random forests, gradient boosting, and many more. Furthermore, Scikit-learn is designed to be fully integrated with the NumPy library.

4. Matplotlib: This open source Python library is designed to add a plotting functionality to the programming language, as well as the NumPy module. This tool is used for visualisation purposes by allowing you to create a plot from certain data, such as an array. In addition, you can interact with the plot directly once created, in the same environment without switching to another application.

These libraries are considered a must have whether you are a beginner machine learner or a professional.

They are all open source and readily available with large, supporting communities built around them. In addition, they are well-documented and have been extensively used to work with real world datasets. This allows you to research other machine learners and see how they applied these tools for their various projects. Never underestimate the power of a popular product. Even if there are better paid ones out there, but they are used only by small groups of people, you should stick with the ones considered as the standard. That way you will always have access to plenty of resources, because you will often need them without a doubt.

Another tool worth mentioning here is Jupyter Notebook, which is similar to an IDE that you may have used when programming. However, it is mostly designed to be used to analyze and process data sets with the help of machine learning algorithms. At first glance, it may look similar to another IDE's such as Visual Studio, however it is quite different. One of the most powerful features it includes is the ability to manipulate plots and visualize them in the same panel where you write all your code. Eliminating the need for other applications and more confusing windows is quite an advantage.

Now that you have some information on the most important tools and you know what they are for, let's explore the final piece of the puzzle, Tensorflow.

## Tensorflow

This is another open source Python-focused library that is designed specifically for machine learning. Keep in mind that machine learning is a complex field and it can be difficult to implement algorithms and training models manually. Fortunately, we have tools like Tensorflow to make our job a whole lot easier. Tensorflow isn't just a simple machine learning library. It is in fact a framework that simplifies nearly every aspect of machine learning, such as data acquisition, model training, serving predictions, and refining results until they are as accurate as possible.

Tensorflow was designed by Google, with the purpose of creating an open source library for complex, large scale machine learning problems. This tool is actually packaged together with a number of machine learning models, as well as neural network models, and a number of algorithms. In other words, TensorFlow provides you with everything you need to train neural networks to classify handwritten digits, perform accurate image recognition, build recurrent neural networks, handle natural language processing and more.

Tensorflow also allows you to create graphs that represent the flow of data. In essence, each graph is a visual structure that shows how the information goes through a number of data processing nodes. Every single node is represented by an operation, and the link between the notes is a multi-dimensional array, also known as a tensor.

All of this functionality is provided through Python. As you already know, this is one of the easiest and most flexible programming languages you can use, and it suits all of your machine learning tasks due its ability to express how to connect complex abstractions together. Therefore we can determine that Tensorflow programs are Python programs. However, take note that the mathematical operations are not performed using Python. Why? Because Tensorflow uses C++ binaries to write the transformations libraries for optimal performance. Python is only used to connect the dots and allow us to use complex programming operations to link all the components together.

Another advantage of working with Tensorflow is that any application you develop with it can run on any computer system. It can run on a local system, the cloud, Android systems, and so on. For instance, you can use Google's cloud service to run the framework together with Google's Tensorflow processing unit. However, the resulting machine learning prediction models will have to be installed on the system they're supposed to run.

Keep in mind that the largest advantage by far is that Tensorflow provides abstraction for our machine learning development projects. This means that you don't have to manually handle the implementation of a machine learning algorithm. You don't even need to know how to set up one function's output to become the input of another function. While you should know how to do all of this because you want to become a machine learner, after all, Tensorflow provides you with the ability to simply place all of your attention on the application itself and not its inner workings. In other words, you deal with the big picture, while Tensorflow works behind the curtain.

In addition, Tensorflow is all about making the developer's life easier. If you develop any applications through this framework you will benefit from debugging them by evaluating every operation individually. You'll be able to analyze the graphs and then edit them as needed instead of reconstructing them from scratch and then performing the analysis again. This way graph visualisation is incredibly interactive and user-friendly, especially when you have full access to the graph and the way it runs through an easy to understand user interface.

A final advantage to this industry standard machine learning library and framework is the fact that Google continues to fuel its development and therefore makes it easier to work with and more powerful with each new version. Furthermore, it becomes much less time consuming to launch it into your development pipeline.

As you can see, there are many advantages to using this tool, however, like any other tool it has its drawbacks. One of the biggest issues is caused by the way Tensorflow is implemented. Some training model results are difficult to extract and we can see this when we train a model on one system and then on another system. The results will vary to some degree.

The problem is that the reason for this is a complicated matter and therefore we can't find a fix-all solution. That is why, to achieve optimal performance and accuracy, you need to know which machine learning techniques to apply, even if you don't do all the dirty work yourself.

# Reinforcement Machine Learning

So far, in this guidebook, we have taken some time to look at what supervised machine learning and unsupervised machine learning are all about. There are a lot of different types of learning algorithms that you are able to work with when you combine these two types of machine learning, and you may find that you are able to get most of the projects that you want to be done with the help of these. But now, it is time to move on to the third type of machine learning, one that can take some of your projects to the next level and may be just what some of your projects are looking for, especially when nothing else seems to work.

The third type of machine learning that we need to take a look at is known as reinforcement learning. These are going to really help you to work on some new projects and will ensure that you are able to finish some work that may not be covered with any of the other options are able to work.

When we first take a look at the idea of reinforcement learning, it is going to carry many of the same similarities that we will find with unsupervised learning as we talked about above. There are some similarities, and until you really get into using them and see the differences, it is hard to understand how these are different.

The first difference that you are going to notice is that the reinforcement machine learning is going to need to have some kind of feedback mechanism that you will need to focus on. If the feedback isn't present, then the learning isn't going to work. You can go through and set these up so that they are either positive or negative, and the choice is going to be determined by the algorithm that you are working with. But regardless of the type of feedback, it needs to be there.

So, any time that you would like to work with one of the algorithms that come with reinforcement machine learning, you are basically working with a program that will focus on trial-and-error-like learning. Think about when you would like to teach a younger child something new.

When this child ends up performing some kind of action or even saying something that is not following the rules or that you don't like, then there is some negative feedback given to them. You may tell them to stop, take away a toy for a bit, or put them on time-out. This teaches the child that the action or the words are not something that they are allowed to work with. Depending on the child, it may take some time and a few tries in order to get this right, but with the consistent punishment or feedback, they will catch on.

The opposite can happen here as well. If the child follows the rules and does what you want, you will need to provide them with some positive feedback as well. You will praise them, offer them something special, or do something else with positive reinforcement to show the child that you approve of what they are doing. Through these two steps, you will find that the child will slowly start to learn the behavior that they are allowed to do and the behavior that they need to avoid.

Of course, while this example is pretty simple, it is a good one to illustrate the way that reinforcement machine learning is able to work. This kind of machine learning is going to follow the idea of trial-and-error but in the programming and coding world. It is going to require that the application is going to follow a specific algorithm that will ensure it can make the best decisions through learning and both the positive and negative feedback.

You will bring up the use of reinforcement machine learning any time that you are going to spend time on a program that needs to make some decisions and you want it to come out with a good outcome without any mistakes. This is going to take you a bit of work and learning before the program can avoid mistakes and learn what you want to do. But this is also something that you are able to add into the code that you want to write to help the code how to work.

Now that we have a brief introduction into what reinforcement learning is, it is time to take a look at some of the learning algorithms that you are able to utilize when it is time to use the features here. Let's get started.

## Q-Learning and How It Works

The first type of reinforcement machine learning that we are going to focus on is going to be known as Q-learning. This is a good learning algorithm to choose if you would like to work with a type of learning that is known as temporal difference learning. As you work with the different machine learning types, you will probably notice that this is one that will be called an off-policy algorithm that has the ability to learn an action value function, which is going to ensure that you are able to get the results that you expect no matter what state the program is in at the time.

One of the nice things about using Q-learning is that you are able to use this algorithm for any of the different functions that you would like. Since this is true, you need to take some time to list out the different specifications for how the user or the learner will select the course of action, or things are going to get split up a bit as well.

After the programmer has time to go through and figure out what the action value function is going to be, then it is time to work with the optimal policy. You are going to be able to come up with that optimal policy by using the actions with the highest value no matter what state you are working with.

There are a lot of different learning algorithms that you are able to work with, but one of the advantages of going with this one is that you won't have to go through and provide it with models of the environment for you to compare the utility of your actions. This is complicated, but what it means is that you are able to compare at least a few, and sometimes many, actions together, and it is going to work no matter what type of environment that is put with it.

## *SARSA*

And the other main type of reinforcement learning that we are going to focus on, even though there are more, is one that is called SARSA. SARSA is short for State Action Reward State Action Algorithm. That is a bit of a mouthful, but that is why we are going to look at the shorter version of it and how you are able to use it for your advantage.

When you have finished with this step, then you have the main function that you would want to use with the updated value. This is going to then rely on whatever the current state of the learner ends up being. It is also going to include some kind of reward that the learner is going to get if they make the right selections and to ensure that you are going to have the program learn along the way.

This already sounds a bit confusing, but it is going to show us that there are a ton of parts that have to come together in some way to ensure that you are able to get the SARSA learning algorithm to work the way that you would like. While there are going to be many different parts that you will be able to come together for this one to work, it is still going to be the safest out of the algorithms for a programmer to use when they are trying to find a solution to solve their problem.

However, this can also be used, because sometimes, there will be a learner who tries to get a reward that is higher than what is seen as average for the work that they did. This is an uneven reward and can make the SARSA algorithm a bit riskier compared to all of the other algorithms that we have talked about in the past.

In addition to this issue, there are going to be a few situations with reinforcement learning where the learner isn't going to be able to follow the optimal path either. Depending on how you have the program set up and how it goes to react with it, it is going to change up the learning process and can make the program not behave in the manner that you would like.

As you can see above, reinforcement machine learning is going to be a bit different compared to what you are going to see with some of the other learning algorithms that we have talked about so far in this guidebook. But this is still one that is unique and that has a lot of applications to make it useful and one that you will want to consider on a regular basis.

With that said, a good way to remember how to work with the ideas of reinforcement machine learning is to remember it is a type of trial-and-error algorithm. It is going to learn how it should behave based on the rewards and consequences of each action. And the more that you stay consistent with this, the easier the program is going to work.

## Package Installation

To get started with NumPy, we have to install the package into our version of Python. While the basic method for installing packages to Python is the **pip install** method, we will be using the **conda install** method. This is the recommended way of managing all

Python packages and virtual environments using the anaconda framework.

Since we installed a recent version of Anaconda, most of the packages we need would have been included in the distribution. To verify if any package is installed, you can use the **conda list** command via the anaconda prompt. This displays all the packages currently installed and accessible via anaconda. If your intended package is not available, then you can install via this method:

First, ensure you have an internet connection. This is required to download the target package via conda. Open the anaconda prompt, then enter the following code:

```
Conda install package
```

> *Note*: In the code above, 'package' is what needs to be installed e.g. NumPy, Pandas, etc.

In programming, an array is an ordered collection of similar items. Sounds familiar? Yeah, they are just like Python lists, but with superpowers. NumPy arrays are in two forms: Vectors, and Matrices. They are mostly the same, only that vectors are one-dimensional arrays (either a column or a row of ordered items), while a matrix is 2-dimensional (rows and columns). These are the fundamental blocks of most operations we would be doing with NumPy. While arrays incorporate most of the operations possible with Python lists, we would be introducing some newer methods for creating, and manipulating them.

To begin using the NumPy methods, we have to first import the package into our current workspace. This can be achieved in two ways:

```
import numpy as np
Or

from numpy import *
```

In Jupyter notebook, enter either of the codes above to import the NumPy package. The first method of import is recommended, especially for beginners, as it helps to keep track of the specific package a called function/method is from. This is due to the variable assignment e.g. 'np', which refers to the imported package throughout the coding session.

Notice the use of an asterisk in the second import method. This signifies 'everything/all' in programming. Hence, the code reads '*from NumPy import everything!!*'

*Tip:* In Python, we would be required to reference the package we are operating with e.g. NumPy, Pandas, etc. It is easier to assign them variable names that can be used in further operations. This is significantly useful in a case where there are multiple packages being used, and the use of standard variable names such as: 'np' for NumPy, 'pd' for Pandas, etc. makes the code more readable.

*Example 55:* Creating vectors and matrices from Python lists.

Let us declare a Python list.

In []: # This is a list of integers
 Int_list = [1,2,3,4,5]
     Int_list

Out[]: [1,2,3,4,5]

Importing the NumPy package and creating an array of integers.

In []: # import syntax
import numpy as np
np.array(Int_list)

Out[]: array([1, 2, 3, 4, 5])

Notice the difference in the outputs? The second output indicates that we have created an array, and we can easily assign this array to a variable for future reference.

To confirm, we can check for the type.

In []: x = np.array(Int_list)

   type(x)

Out[]: numpy.ndarray

We have created a vector, because it has one dimension (1 row). To check this, the 'ndim' method can be used.

In []: x.ndim    # this shows how many dimensions the array has

Out[]: 1

Alternatively, the shape method can be used to see the arrangements.

In []: x.shape   # this shows the shape

Out[]: (5,)

Python describes matrices as **(rows, columns)**. In this case, it describes a vector as **(number of elements, )**.

To create a matrix from a Python list, we need to pass a nested list containing the elements we need. Remember, matrices are rectangular, and so each list in the nested list must have the same size.

In []: # This is a matrix

```python
x = [1,2,3]
y = [4,5,6]
my_list = [y,x]  # nested list
my_matrix = np.array(my_list)  # creating the
    matrix
A = my_matrix.ndim
B = my_matrix.shape
# Printing
print('Resulting
    matrix:\n\n',my_matrix,'\n\nDimensions:',A,
'\nshape (rows,columns):',B)
```

Out[]: Resulting matrix:

[[4 5 6]

[1 2 3]]

Dimensions: 2

shape (rows,columns): (2, 3)

Now, we have created a 2 by 3 matrix. Notice how the shape method displays the rows and columns of the matrix. To find the transpose of this matrix i.e. change the rows to columns, use the **transpose ()** method.

```python
In []: # this finds the transpose of the matrix
t_matrix = my_matrix.transpose()
    t_matrix
```

Out[]: array([[4, 1],

```
    [5, 2],
    [6, 3]])
```

*Tip:* Another way of knowing the number of dimensions of an array is by counting the square-brackets that opens and closes the array (immediately after the parenthesis). In the vector example, notice that the array was enclosed in single square brackets. In the two-dimensional array example, however, there are two brackets. Also, tuples can be used in place of lists for creating arrays.

There are other methods of creating arrays in Python, and they may be more intuitive than using lists in some application. One quick method uses the **arange()** function.

- Syntax: np.arange(start value, stop value, step size, dtype = 'type')

This method is similar to the **range()** method we used in example 43. In this case, we do not need to pass its output to the list function, our result is an array object of a data type specified by 'dtype'.

*Example 56*: Creating arrays with the arange() function.

We will create an array of numbers from 0 to 10, with an increment of 2 (even numbers).

In []: # Array of even numbers between 0 and 10
Even_array = np.arange(0,11,2)
Even_array

Out[]: array([ 0, 2, 4, 6, 8, 10])

Notice it behaves like the range () method form our list examples. It returned all even values between 0 and 11 (10 being the maximum). Here, we did not specify the types of the elements.

> *Tip:* Recall, the range method returns value up to the 'stop value – 1'; hence, even if we change the 11 to 12, we would still get 10 as the maximum.

Since the elements are numeric, they can either be integers or floats. Integers are the default, however, to return the values as floats, we can also specify the numeric type.

In []: Even_array2 = np.arange(0,11,2, dtype='float')

Even_array2

Out[]: array([ 0., 2., 4., 6., 8., 10.])

Another handy function for creating arrays is **linspace()**. This returns a numeric array of linearly space values within an interval. It also allows for the

126

specification of the required number of points, and it has the following syntax:

```
np.linspace(start value, end value, number of points)
```

At default, linspace returns an array of 50 evenly spaced points within the defined interval.

*Example 57*: Creating arrays of evenly spaced points with linspace()

In []: # Arrays of linearly spaced points
A = np.linspace(0,5,5) # 5 equal points between 0 & 5
B = np.linspace (51,100) # 50 equal points between
        51 & 100
    print ('Here are the arrays:\n')

A

B

Here are the arrays:

Out[ ]: array([0.  , 1.25, 2.5 , 3.75, 5. ])
Out[ ]: array([ 1.,  2.,  3.,  4.,  5.,  6.,  7.,  8.,  9.,
        10., 11., 12., 13., 14., 15., 16., 17., 18., 19.,
        20., 21., 22., 23., 24., 25., 26., 27., 28., 29.,
        30., 31., 32., 33., 34., 35., 36., 37., 38., 39.,
        40., 41., 42., 43., 44., 45., 46., 47., 48., 49.,
        50.])

Notice how the second use of linspace did not require a third argument. This is because we wanted 50 equally spaced values, which is the default. The 'dtype' can also be specified like we did with the range function.

> *Tip 1:* Linspace arrays are particularly useful in plots. They can be used to create a time axis or any other required axis for producing well defined and scaled graphs.

> *Tip 2:* The output format in the example above is not the default way for output in Jupyter notebook. Jupyter displays the last result per cell, at default. To display multiple results (without having to use the print statement every-time), the output method can be changed using the following code.

```
In[]: # Allowing Jupyter output all results per cell.
# run the following code in a Jupyter cell.
from IPython.core.interactiveshell import InteractiveShell

InteractiveShell.ast_node_interactivity = "all"
```

There are times when a programmer needs unique arrays like the identity matrix, or a matrix of ones/zeros. NumPy provides a convenient way of creating these with the **zeros()**, **ones()** and **eye()** functions.

*Example 58:* creating arrays with unique elements.

Let us use the zeros () function to create a vector and a matrix.

# In []: np.zeros(3)  # A vector of 3 elements
# np.zeros((2,3)) # A matrix of 6 elements i.e. 2 rows, 3 columns

Out[]: array([0., 0., 0.])

Out[]: array([[0., 0., 0.],

   [0., 0., 0.]])

Notice how the second output is a two-dimensional array i.e. two square brackets (a matrix of 2 columns and 3 rows as specified in the code).

The same thing goes for creating a vector or matrix with all elements having a value of '1'.

In []: np.ones(3)  # A vector of 3 elements

 np.ones((2,3)) # A matrix of 6 elements i.e. 2 rows, 3 columns

Out[]: array([1., 1., 1.])

Out[]: array([[1., 1., 1.],

   [1., 1., 1.]])

Also, notice how the code for creating the matrices requires the row and column instructions to be passed as a tuple. This is because the function accepts one input, so multiple inputs would need to be passed as tuples or lists in the required order (Tuples are recommended. Recall, they are faster to operate.).

In the case of the identity matrix, the function eye () only requires one value. Since identity matrices are always square, the value passed determines the number of rows and columns.

In []: np.eye(2)  # A matrix of 4 elements 2 rows, 2
    columns
 np.eye(3)  # 3 rows, 3 columns
Out[]: array([[1., 0.],
       [0., 1.]])
Out[]: array([[1., 0., 0.],
       [0., 1., 0.],
       [0., 0., 1.]])

NumPy also features random number generators. These can be used for creating arrays, as well as single values, depending on the required application. To access the random number generator, we call the library via **np.random**, and then choose the random method we prefer. We will consider three methods for generating random numbers: **rand()**, **randn()**, and **randint()**.

*Example 59:* Generating arrays with random values.

Let us start with the rand () method. This generates random, uniformly distributed numbers between 0 and 1.

**In []: np.random.rand (2)    # A vector of 2 random values**

**np.random.rand (2,3)  # A matrix of 6 random values**

**Out[]: array([0.01562571, 0.54649508])**

**Out[]: array([[0.22445055, 0.35909056, 0.53403529],**

[0.70449515, 0.96560456, 0.79583743]])

Notice how each value within the arrays are between 0 & 1. You can try this on your own and observe the returned values. Since it is a random generation, these values may be different from yours. Also, in the case of the random number generators, the matrix specifications are not required to be passed as lists or tuples, as observed in the second line of code.

The randn () method generates random numbers from the standard normal or Gaussian distribution. You might want to brush up on some basics in statistics, however, this just implies that the values returned would have a tendency towards the mean (which is zero in this case) i.e. the values would be centered around zero.

In []: np.random.randn (2)     # *A vector of 2 random values*

np.random.randn (2,3)   # *A matrix of 6 random values*

Out[]: array([ 0.73197866, -0.31538023])

Out[]:     array([[-0.79848228,    -0.7176693    ,
    0.74770505],
    [-2.10234448,  0.10995745, -0.54636425]])

The randint() method generates random integers within a specified range or interval. Note that the higher range value is exclusive (i.e. has no chance of being randomly selected), while the lower value is inclusive (could be included in the random selection).

- Syntax:  np.random(lower value, higher value, number of values, dtype)

If the number of values is not specified, Python just returns a single value within the defined range.

In []: np.random.randint (1,5)     # *A random value between 1 and 5*

np.random.randint (1,100,6)     # *A vector of 6 random values* np.random.randint (1,100,(2,3)) # A matrix of 6 random values

Out[]: 4

Out[]: array([74, 42, 92, 10, 76, 43])

Out[]: array([[92, 9, 99],
          [73, 36, 93]])

*Tip:* Notice how the size parameter for the third line was specified using a tuple. This is how to create a matrix of random integers using randint.

*Example 59*: Illustrating randint().

Let us create a fun dice roll program using the randint() method. We would allow two dice, and the function will return an output based on the random values generated in the roll.

In []: # creating a dice roll game with randint()
 # Defining the function
 def roll_dice():
        """ This function displays a
        dice roll value when called"""
  dice1 = np.random.randint(1,7) # *This allows 6 to be inclusive*
       dice2 = np.random.randint(1,7)
# Display Condition.
       if dice1 == dice2:

```
        print('Roll: ',dice1,'&',dice2,'\ndoubles !')

            if dice1 == 1:

                print('snake eyes!\n')

        else:

            print('Roll: ',dice1,'&',dice2)
```

In []: # Calling the function

 roll_dice()

Out[]: Roll:  1 & 1

doubles !

snake eyes!

> *Hint:* Think of a fun and useful program to illustrate the use of these random number generators, and writing such programs will improve your chances of comprehension. Also, a quick review of statistics, especially measures of central tendency & dispersion/spread will be useful in your data science journey.

# Predictive Analytics

- In this chapter, we will investigate an area of data analysis called predictive analytics. More than fifty years ago, we learned about predictive analytics from Hollywood and the science fiction author Arthur C. Clarke in the story 2001: A Space Odyssey. In the movie, everything appears to be running fine, but the artificially intelligent computer detects a pending failure in a communications unit. The computer even tells us when the unit will fail. When the unit is removed and studied, the astronauts discover it is not defective, calling into question the previously unquestioned capabilities of the computer.

That part is not relevant for our discussion, but the point of this story is that it had the basic concept of predictive analytics in mind. That is, trying to anticipate and/or prevent some future event based on data regarding a device, customer, or patient.

Predictive analytics is anticipated to have applications in many areas, and as the field is developed, interest by large corporations, sporting organizations, manufacturers, and governments are sure to be high. We will explain what predictive analytics is, who uses it, how it is used, and how it is tied to big data.

## What is Predictive Analytics?

The purpose of predictive analytics is to make predictions about future events, which can have wide applications. For example, the manufacturer of an aircraft might want to predict an engine failure. On the other hand, a service like Netflix might want to predict when a subscriber will cancel their service.

If you run a hedge fund or large stock brokerage, you might be interested in learning what signs occur in market data just before a bear market crash. Medical professionals studying cardiovascular disease could be interested in determining if changes occur in certain blood markers when a heart attack is imminent. Another example could be used in the financial world. Credit card or loan companies might look for behavior patterns that occur just before a person will default on a loan.

In each case, the problems seem very different at first glance, but they have a lot in common—looking for certain patterns in the data that will be a precursor to the event they wish to analyze. For example, on Netflix, you might find certain changes to watching patterns. Maybe the frequency with which the app is opened decreases below a certain threshold. Or users may still open the app, but they may spend more time browsing rather than selecting shows or movies to watch.

With predictive analytics, you will be looking for certain factors to come together to indicate that such an event is about to occur. Before doing any analysis, we might not know what those factors are. In the discussion about Netflix, we are merely speculating. That kind of guesswork is not the kind of information that companies are after today, so they need to use big data to get the answers.

To determine what factors need to come together for the event we want to predict, large amounts of data should be collected and analyzed. The benefit is that you will find many past failures. Continuing to use Netflix as an example, they have tens of millions of subscribers, so there is ample data to analyze the behavior of people who canceled their subscriptions.

## Why Use Predictive Analytics?

The purpose of using predictive analytics is so that companies can adopt a proactive stance. That is, they need to take action before the event happens. There is nothing magical going on here. When the company can proactively deal with the situation, then it can intervene before the failure or service cancellation occurs.

In the case of the airplane engine, the plane can be grounded and send for an inspection. The patterns that might emerge when studying past engine failures might provide the information necessary to enact appropriate repairs. An engine failure won't happen unexpectedly, even if before doing your analysis you do not know what systems within the engine tend to fail. This information may be learned using the tools of predictive analytics. With this information in hand, the company can enact repairs on those systems to significantly lower the probability of engine failure.

In the case of behavior that predicts default on a loan, the company could contact the customer to make new payment arrangements to avoid the default. The Netflix example is very common today. Netflix will be very interested in determining if someone is likely to consider canceling their subscription. If they can get this information, then they can take action to try to keep the subscriber. They can start presenting the customer with renewal offers that propose a discount if they renew their subscription within a limited time period. This proactive stance would help the company avoid losing large numbers of users.

## The Role of Statistics

The science fiction example we began the chapter with had important information in it. This type of approach in real life won't be considered a success or failure when applied to a sample size of one. Continuing with the Netflix example, we obviously can't deem the data correct if one subscriber predicted to cancel doesn't do so, or if another that didn't meet the criteria ends up canceling. This is a phenomenon rooted in statistics. It will give probabilities and will only have meaning when applied to large numbers of cases, possibly on the order of tens of thousands or more. The more people you apply this to, the more accurate the prediction will be.

The best we could hope for is something akin to the following. Maybe Netflix identifies five behaviors that tend to come together when a subscriber will cancel within thirty days. However, it is not an absolute rule. It might tell you that there is a 90 percent chance the subscriber will cancel, and perhaps subscribers who showed four, or fewer, or even none of the behaviors would cancel. Maybe if the subscriber only exhibits four of the behaviors, there is a 75 percent chance of cancellation. If they show none of the behaviors, there could be a 15 percent chance of cancellation. These examples illustrate how predictive analytics could be applied in practice to avert an undesirable event.

## How to Generate Predictions

Now let us consider how we go about getting that information in the first place.

We must start with a source of data. Predictive analytics works best with structured data, but it can work with unstructured data as well. To provide accurate predictions, large amounts of data are required. In statistics, we know that the more data you collect, the more accurate your relationships will. If you are not an expert in statistics, you can see this when polls are taken for political elections. Any poll that does not report the amount of error should be immediately ignored, but most of them will tell you that the results could vary by +/- 3 percent or something to this effect. A poll that showed candidate A was leading candidate B by 49 percent–47 percent, with a margin of error of +/- 3 percent, would be completely worthless. This is because the data could be wrong, and the real result could shift up by 3 percent or down by 3 percent in a variety of ways. To be significant, the difference between the candidates would have to be larger than the error. If the same poll had instead found A to be leading B by a margin of 52 percent to 47 percent, we could take those results more seriously. The other result would indicate that the race was tied.

Something else you will notice about political polls is the larger the sample size, the more accurate the poll results. This is because the margin of error and the sample size are inversely related. You can consult your favorite statistics book to see the specific mathematical formulas if you are interested in the details.

The point is that we need big data. Companies have the data on hand, but they won't be willing to take action based on information that has a large amount of error in today's environment.

## Enter Machine Learning

We cover more details about machine learning in a later chapter, but it could play a leading role in predictive analytics. Machine learning can help us find patterns and relationships in any big data we already have. With predictive analytics, this is exactly what we need. For example, Netflix collects information about its subscribers every time you use—and even do not use—Netflix on your television or other devices. This not only includes how often you open the application but what you do once you open it. It tracks what you watch and records other behaviors as well, such as whether the user immediately opens a popular Netflix program or searches for an older movie or TV program. Nearly a million questions could be asked, and Netflix probably has all the answers within their reams of data.

This is a classic big data problem. Not all the data collected from tens of millions of people will be something engineers can look at in a spreadsheet and provide the answers management is seeking. It will require computer power to analyze it.

Machine learning can be used to train a computer system. For example, Netflix would feed a computer data on the viewing habits of people who have already canceled their subscriptions. Then the computer would be unleashed to evaluate the data to discover hidden patterns, trends, and relationships between different behaviors or factors not immediately obvious to human eyes.

Before the data is analyzed, we could not possibly know what the factors are. Once machine learning has been used to train the computer system to find out what they are, then the computer can be used to analyze data coming in from existing users. From here, it can flag users who meet the criteria. This will allow Netflix to take action to try to prevent the subscriber from canceling.

## Product Improvement

Predictive analytics also has other advantages. Such an analysis might reveal how a product or service could be improved. Rather than waiting for someone to get to the point of canceling their subscription, Netflix might see what factors are causing people to cancel and then make changes to their service to better meet customer demands.

This approach can be used in any situation. Consider the previous example of an engine failure on an aircraft. Over the short term, the factors that precede engine failure could be used to ground a plane and bring it in for an inspection and possible repairs. Over the long term, the design of the engine could be modified. The modification would proceed based on the new knowledge of what system failures were occurring prior to an actual engine failure. More robust systems could be designed, or specific components could be redesigned to increase the reliability of the system as a whole.

## Benefits of Predictive Analytics

Predictive analytics won't create completely flawless systems. However, before predictive analytics and big data, companies had to act based on very limited information and relied on educated guesses and hunches. As a result, the efficiency in operations, reliability in products, and quality of services were not nearly as good as it could be.

Although predictive analytics cannot provide you with 100 percent reliability (nothing can do that anyway), it takes guessing out of the process. Over time, predictive analytics can also be refined. If a company can predict failure to a 90 percent probability, in a few years, they may be able to push that to 95 percent or higher. The more data the company can collect, the more the predictive analytical tools can be refined and improved.

The result is that there will be many benefits both to the company and to the people they serve. First, companies that manufacture products can build products that are safer, more reliable, and offer better performance, overall. Those that offer services can improve them to better meet the needs of their customer base.

Suppose Netflix found that customers who are likely to cancel skip the screen showing current, popular Netflix programs and instead immediately search for movies shown in theaters. Netflix could improve its service by identifying which behavior a user is more likely to engage in. They could then personalize the startup screen seen by each user to better meet their needs.

## The Process of Predictive Analytics

The predictive analytics process will move through many stages. Like any activity within a large organization, it will begin by defining the problem. The problem must be defined precisely so that models and computer systems have something specific to tackle, and all members of the organization understand the goals. The scope of the effort should be more limited to get more reliable results.

Once the problem has been identified, big data comes in. This is where the role of the data scientist becomes more important. Data scientists in the organization must determine the best data sources to tackle and solve the problem.

Data has often already been collected, but, if necessary, there can be a data collection stage. In some cases, the need for certain data may be identified in the planning stage. While this will cause some delays in moving forward, if the data is required for a solution to the problem, this step will be essential.

Once the data sets are selected or become available, the data science team can begin a preliminary analysis. This will include the framing of hypotheses and preliminary modeling. Various algorithms are available to use with machine learning that we will go over later in the book. For now, just be aware that the data science team would analyze the data to determine which algorithms are most suitable to get the results they are seeking.

Next, the test data will be selected, and the type selected will depend on many factors. For example, you will have some known data in some cases. This could be the case for a subscription service like Netflix. Certainly, the company would have information that would include subscribers who have canceled their service. The company may even have survey data from a subset of users. Some companies may attempt to ask users some simple questions to get at the reasons for cancellation. A preliminary examination of the data may also reveal some inputs that correlate to the output at hand, which is canceling the service. However, that data may not be available, but it does not matter because machine learning can proceed either way.

The next step is to train the system on subsets of data. This is the learning phase of machine learning. The system will be presented with data, and it will seek out patterns, correlations, and trends that can be used for future estimates.

At each step, the data science team will analyze the results, and the learning process can continue until the team is satisfied with the current state of performance.

At this point, the models can be deployed in real time. Netflix models can be used to read data from customers as it's coming in, and they predict future cancellations.

## Prescriptive Analytics

As the model is in operation, the results will be evaluated on a continual basis to look for areas of improvement. A process called prescriptive analytics can be used to analyze the performance of the model and update it if necessary to improve performance. It can also be used to respond to changing conditions in real time. Keep in mind that changes are always happening in today's fast-paced world.

## Applications of Predictive Analytics

As we have shown, businesses and other large organizations can use predictive analytics in many ways. Some of the applications can be quite surprising, but applications of big data usually are. Let us familiarize ourselves with some general applications of predictive analytics.

## Healthcare

The function of predictive analytics in healthcare are quite numerous. One common problem that occurs in hospitals is secondary infections. Patients might come in with a viral or other illness and then contract bacterial pneumonia while in the hospital. This problem is ripe for machine learning, provided that the data is available. Big data could be used in conjunction with machine learning to develop models that would estimate a patient's risk for developing secondary infections. The hospital could take steps to reduce the risk, such as keeping patient exposure to others at a minimum during their hospital stay. Nursing and other healthcare staff could also implement extra protection and handwashing measures.

Another application in the healthcare arena is determining who is at risk for different diseases before symptoms occur. For example, patients could be analyzed to determine their risk of developing diabetes or heart disease. Big data analytics could be used to find patterns in the data for breast and prostate cancer, identifying patients that are at high risk of developing these diseases using previously unknown hidden patterns so that intervention or additional screening could be applied.

Both big data and predictive analytics can be used to improve staffing in hospitals. For example, we could determine the best times or days to increase staffing using predictive analytics and determine where to allocate that staffing.

## Customer Relations

Predictive analytics could be used in many other ways for customer relations. For example, using data from previous customer calls, predictive analytics can predict when a customer is about to become irate and cause difficulties for customer service personnel. A series of steps could then be developed to diffuse the situation and help the customer feel they are receiving good customer service.

# Data Science in Weather Patterns

Various weather satellites and sensors are currently orbiting the world. That means a lot of weather data is being collected on a daily basis. This data is then used for monitoring all weather conditions.

The data that gets collected is due to data science playing a big role in the following ways:

- Accurate weather predictions
- Studying and monitoring of global warming
- Monitoring and analyzing natural disaster patterns
- Developing emergency preparedness plans
- Predicting when usable water is available for drought areas

*Example*

IBM's Deep Thunder technology is an ongoing research endeavor that conducts highly accurate forecasting by using data science. IBM has also been busy in Tokyo for improving the forecasting of weather.

Data Science in Transportation

Ever since data science has been in use, it has been very detrimental throughout the transportation industry. Not only has it made it efficient, but have also played a major role in the following ways:

- **Planning of routes**

Data science is used in the planning of routes based on the needs of users that are taking certain routes or using different modes of travel.

- **Management of Congestion and traffic control**

The use of data science can provide a real-time prediction of traffic congestion as well as the times of day when congestion will be worst. We see this already in use via the use of Google Maps.

- **Amount of Traffic Safety**

Data science provides real-time analysis to determine areas that are more prone to accidents. This will ultimately reduce the number of accidents while increasing safety.

*Example*

A good example of this is Uber. Uber utilizes a ton of data regarding its drivers, locations, vehicles, and trip data. This data then gets analyzed and is used to measure supply and demand, locate drivers, and calculate future fare prices.

Data Science in Banking

The banking and finance field is booming with data and is predicted to grow by at least 200 percent by 2020. Having good analysis will help in the detection of fraud and all other activities concerning money like:

- Credit/debit card fraud
- Counterfeiting
- Business clarity
- Alteration of customer statistics
- Money laundering
- Risk mitigation

**Example**

There are many types of software used to deter money laundering including one called SAS AML that uses data analytics to monitor transactions that seem suspicious and then analyzing the customer data.

Introduction of: Data Analytics, Big Data, Data Mining, Computer Science and its Applications in Business

## Data Analytics

Data analytics, or DA for short, is a method used to examine multiple sets of data to be able to form a conclusion generated out of their information. The techniques and technologies of data analytics are used widely among the commercial industry so that companies can then make informed decisions based on research so that it can be either verified or disproved as an effective model, hypothesis, or theory.

Inside the data analytics process

The process of analytics involves a process of data collection where a data scientist will help to identify information needed for an application of analytics, then when done, they go and work on the application alone or together with a data engineer. If data comes from a system of different source, then it may have to be combined using a data integration routine that gets transformed through common formats and then loaded inside of an analytics system like a Hadoop, data warehouse, or a NoSQL database. For other purposes, the process of collection may include pulling of subsets that are relevant from a stream of data that is raw and flows into a Hadoop and then moves to a partition that is separate from the system, so it will be easily analyzed without the data set being affected overall.

## Big Data

To understand what big data is, it is good to know some of its background histories. So, according to the definition found in Gartner (which is still the most current definition): Big data is a kind of data that has a wider variety of data that shows up in great amounts and an even fiercer amount of velocity.

Simply put, this big data is 5 times larger and has data sets that have a higher amount of complexity that stems from newly formed sources of data. With these new sets of data, they are so jam-packed with data that the software used for traditional processing of data is simply unable to manage it all. The good thing is that the amount of data can address problems in business that would not have been addressed beforehand.

## Big Data's History

The original idea for big data is still fairly new, although big data's main origins stem as far back as the '60s while data was just getting created and organized in the very first data center along with a rational database becoming developed.

In 2005, it was starting to be realized that a large amount of data was being generated through the social networks of YouTube, Twitter, and Facebook. This was the same year that Hadoop (a framework that is open-sourced to analyze and store huge data sets) became developed. We also saw NoSQL become popular at this point, too.

When these frameworks for open-source were developed, they became essential for big data's growth due to their ability to make storage cheaper and work easier. In the years to follow, big data did nothing but skyrocket. With many users continuing to generate this data, it seems to have no end in sight. But, humans are not the only ones who are generating this big data. When the Internet of Things was created, many devices and objects got connected and immediately began to gather big data concerning the usage pattern of customers and the products overall performance. With the introduction of machine learning, the amount of data produced continues to grow.

Big data has come a long way, and the full use of it is only at its infancy.

With the expansion of computing being generated in the Cloud, this creates even more possibilities for big data to go farther. With the Cloud being scalable, developers can easily create clusters of ad hoc if they want to test data subsets.

**Data Mining**

With data mining, we are using a process that analyzes a data's hidden pattern by using various perspectives of categorization of information that is useful, assembled, and collected in a common area, like a warehouse for data, to be analyzed efficiently, algorithms for data mining, business decision-making facilitation, and various other requirements that will finally conduct cost-cutting and have revenue increased.

It is known also as knowledge discovery or data discovery.

There are four major steps that are involved in the process of data mining and they are:

- The extraction, transforming, and loading of data into big data warehouses.
- Managing and storing of data in Cloud databases.
- Access of data is provided to analysts via a software application.
- Data that is analyzed is presented in an easy to understand way.

Data mining begins by gathering data that is both relevant and business-critical. Data that concerns a company is considered to be metadata, non-operational, or transactional. With transactional data, this is the daily dealings of the business like cost, inventory, and sales. Data that is non-operational is considered forecast, and metadata involves a database's logical design. Data elements containing relationships and patterns are then able to render information that is relevant, thus increasing the revenue of an organization. When a business has a strong focus on consumers by using the techniques of data mining, they are able to provide a visualization of the products that were sold, the product's price, the demographics of the customer, and competition information.

An example of this is WalMart. This giant retailer is able to transmit relevant information to a big data warehouse using terabytes. It can then be accessed easily by a supplier that can enable them the power to identify the purchasing patterns of a customer. These shopping patterns involve the most days shopped, most products sought after as well as other data that data mining can recognize.

Second, an algorithm that is suitable for data mining must be selected. This algorithm must then be able to identify trends in a data set and use the output to define a parameter. With the algorithms that are more popular, they are used for relationship identification in the elements of the data. With vendors like SQL and Oracle, the data mining incorporates an algorithm like a regression tree or clustering so that the data mine's demand is met.

## *Computer Science and its Applications in Business*

Ever since the invention of the computer, they have changed the lives of many people in a dramatic way. In business, they have also made big impacts on operations. So much so, that anybody who has a computer science degree can easily land a job in just about any field. Also, if you are more of the entrepreneurial type, then a computer science degree would make a great tool in opening your own business.

## Development of Software

All computers are software-driven; this is why a degree in computer science is largely made up of the software being understood. With software, there is a lot that goes into it including an operating system that is big enough to handle the data or a simple app that is downloadable to a smartphone. Having a wide range of options also provides opportunities for the creation of a successful software company. Or perhaps, you want to help others so you decide to write your own software that is practical enough for others to use. Or, how about you develop the next big hit in apps or video games? You can even collaborate with customers to develop content that is customized to their needs.

## Development of Web

Today, it seems like everybody wants to look available while being online. This explains why the field of web development is so popular. Not only can a company develop, maintain, and upload websites for other companies, but they can also personalize them for individual clientele. If you plan on expanding you can easily upgrade to utilize SEO and other tactics that improve an online presence.

As website demand continues to grow, a company specializing in web development becomes an even better option for those wishing to major in computer science. A lot of people already have the fundamental skills to create a website, but what they don't have is the advanced knowledge to be able to code or implement the code.

## IT Support

As more computers and electronic gadgets get used on a daily basis, they will also need more support in maintaining their equipment.

With computers being very useful, they can cause major problems if they stop functioning. While several companies hire staff made up of IT professionals, a smaller business will most likely use outsourcing. With a bigger pool of clients available due to the number of devices, a business specializing in IT support can collaborate with many different brands to either provide direct services or be more widespread with offering support based on interests.

## *Marketing*

Marketing has now become a part of the business. So, this means computer science can now be a part of the marketing business. This is good for all parties involved because a web developer can easily make a marketer visible online in all types of media including their own personal website. You will be helping marketers get their name and brand out there by using the available tools only found online. These include campaigns on social media and email marketing and all of which are seen as important in today's world of marketing.

## Internet Marketplace

If you plan to open a business online, then your degree in computer science can also assist in the creation of your online store. Regardless of the items, you wish to sell, your degree will allow you to open an appealing website that includes a profitable online store.

Overcoming demands for technicalities raised by online stores can be more difficult than it is realized, so if the power is available for website maintenance, then you should be able to save a lot of costs so that your business can be streamlined.

## Basic Terminology in Data Science

If you are just getting started in the world of data science, you should be aware that you will experience many overwhelming periods. This plays especially true for those of you who will use the many techniques and concepts required by a data scientist in order to perform at peak performance. Even the "data science" term can seem pretty vague, so as data science continues to become popular, it will also start to become less defined.

But luckily for you, we have created a list of data science terminology for your reference. Hopefully, you will get great use out of it and be able to refer back to it when you need a term clarified.

### *Fundamentals*

Fundamentals are baseline concepts that can be helpful as you start your data science career.

Although you might not see yourself working with each of these concepts, it is good to know the terms especially when you see yourself reading technical manuals or while talking about the field with fellow data heads.

## Algorithms

Algorithms are sets of certain instructions that a computer is given for it to manipulate values. thus allowing them to be usable. An algorithm can be created to complete many diverse jobs that range from high difficulty to very minimal.

## Back End

A back end is a technology and code that is involved but is never seen and used for populating the information that is useful for the front end. These include procedures for authentication, servers, and databases.

## Big Data

The term big data refers to data that is almost too much for it all to be used. The thing about big data is that it is based more on the tools and strategies that assist computers with the analysis of large data sets. For problems to be addressed using big data, they must be in one of these four categories: velocity, variety, volume, and veracity.

*Classification*

The term classification is a problem associated with supervised machine learning. Its function is to help in categorizing data points by using similarities from other data points. The process works by taking a data set that is categorized and find if any commonalities exist between the two.

*Database*

A database is exactly what the name implies, a space for data storage. A database is widely used with DBMS's (Database Management System). A database is referred to as a computer application that enables the user to have an interaction with databases in order to have the information analyzed after being collected.

Data Warehouse

Data warehouses are systems that are used for rapid analysis for many trends in business that come from other sources. A data warehouse is designed to allow normal people the chance to provide an answer to a statistical question.

## Front End

A front end is what the customer sees and directly interacts with. This could include web pages, forms, or dashboards.

# Conclusion

Thank you for taking the time to read this exciting book about big data. I'd like to conclude by talking a bit about the implications of the big data revolution we are experiencing. There are two main threads that fit into this discussion. The first one is the possibility of massive job losses and upheaval of the economy as a result of these new technologies. The second thread involves privacy issues.

When we think about new technology, we tend to think in terms of gadgets. The first thing that might come to mind is your cell phone. Self-driving cars, spaceflight, and other technologies that you can hold in your hand or see also intrigue us.

For this reason, big data is an unusual development in the history of technology. It is largely unseen by the general public even though you are feeling its effects. Also, in the process of analyzing big data, there are analysts, statistical models, fast computer systems, along with a large computer storage systems and cloud computing. If people think about it at all, they would probably be focused on the computers themselves. However, it is the data on the hard drives and the software algorithms that analyze that data which is important.

When you consider all the technologies that have been developed in the last fifty years, many of them pale in significance compared to big data. For example, think of all the attention that has been lavished on cell phones. For all the wonder that a device like an iPhone provides, its impact on society at large won't be near the impact from big data and machine learning.

For example, a smartphone is unlikely to cause you to lose your job. However, big data in machine learning may do exactly that. Whether that matters to you, one thing we know for certain is that possibly millions of jobs will be eliminated over a very short time. It is too early to determine what the impact of this will be. In several instances in the past, new technologies have created far more jobs than they destroyed. In fact, that has always been the case ever since the Industrial Revolution started. We already talked about the example of the textile machines and the Luddites, but there are even more recent examples. Those under the age of forty probably are not aware of what life was like prior to the massive adoption of computer systems. In the 1970s and even into the 1980s, many businesses did spreadsheet work by hand. Secretaries were used to typing documents on typewriters.

At that time, spreadsheet programs and word processors we are rapidly gaining the market share as businesses adopted them. This scared many people at the time.

People imagined that the office would soon become free of paper and that the advent of spreadsheets and word processors would eliminate millions of jobs.

The same thing happened the more these technologies became used in more and more offices. Rather than eliminate jobs, the impact was to create millions of new jobs instead. This happens because productivity is massively increased with each introduction of new technology. Second, it frees people from trivial tasks they were devoting their time to before. A strange thing happens as these patterns develop. People find out that new must-do and must-have things become required in the new economy that springs out of the chaos.

That is likely to be the case this time as well. Although robotics will certainly eliminate many jobs, new jobs that you cannot even imagine right now will spring up in their place. Some people cite the rapid pace of transformation as a reason to be pessimistic about this. However, it should be noted that this will also cause an explosion in the pace of change, which brings about an entirely new business in place of the old jobs lost to robotics and artificial intelligence.

Another thing that happens during a transformation process like this is that the economy itself grows by a large amount, so even if you lost a certain number of jobs, the growth of the economy, which is benefiting from the new technologies, will more than offset the loss of those jobs. There will always be jobs for humans to perform, so people might be doing new things, but they will certainly have some things to do.

In fact, we are already seeing this on a large-scale. When the internet became available to the general public and to businesses, it created many new jobs and job categories that did not exist before. This was also accompanied by changes generated by the existence of software programs such as Photoshop. Some new job categories that have proven very lucrative include web programmers, graphic designers, JavaScript programmers, and so forth. This has also happened with respect to mobile or smartphones. It is estimated that as a result of the iPhone, there are 1.5 million new jobs in the United States. These jobs are related to app development and include computer programming jobs, user interface design, graphic design, as well as millions of people who have started their own businesses centered on developing iPhone apps. The numbers are probably even larger when you consider Google's Android.

In addition, the video gaming industry is growing in leaps and bounds. Games continue to be developed for traditional devices like consoles, but many companies are only developing games for use on smartphones. This has created an entirely new set of job possibilities.

In my view, something similar will happen as artificial intelligence, big data, and machine learning continue to weave their way throughout our society.

Regarding the privacy issue, privacy and ethical concerns are certainly important. However, it is my opinion that big data has already won the day and won't go away anytime soon. In fact, the importance of big data will increase in the coming years, and its commercial impact is too large for companies to ignore. Not only does selling data provide a lucrative way to generate income, but big data also increases the power of marketing and advertising as well as customer service for large corporations. The benefits of this are just way too large, and no matter what politicians do, I don't believe they can stop this process.

With that in mind, we must consider protecting our own data, becoming more aware of the terms of service and privacy rules, and being more concerned about security. One factor that has made data sharing controversial is a simple fact people do not pay attention to. It is painful, but you must take the time to read software company documents regarding privacy. If Congress will do anything, it might be helpful if they would require companies to present clear and easy-to-understand information related to these issues that could be read quickly by customers. Think about what happens nine times out of ten when people open a website or app and are faced with terms of service or privacy agreements. Most people are far too impatient to deal with this, and the legalese of these documents simply gives them a headache. So they quickly dismiss the document by agreeing to it. If you are engaging in that type of behavior, you cannot blame Facebook, Google, or any of the other big tech companies if you find out later that your data was shared.

Politicians are probably mistaken if they believe they will solve this problem by breaking up the big tech companies. Big data will still be there, and it will be worth more than ever if that happens. In my opinion, it is probably better to have a few powerful companies managing and controlling a large fraction of the data. In any case, if they break up these companies, the problem will just shift around rather than go away. It might also be harder for governments to regulate, which would defeat their purpose. I tend to take a libertarian view as long as there is not abuse, so in my opinion, the company should not be broken up. However, there should be some simple regulations put in place to ensure that people can protect their privacy. Data sharing should be allowed, but no one should be able to identify specific individuals in that data.